The
Great
Money
Reset

ALSO BY JILL SCHLESINGER

*The Dumb Things Smart People
Do with Their Money*

The
Great
Money
Reset

CHANGE YOUR WORK
CHANGE YOUR WEALTH
CHANGE YOUR LIFE

Jill Schlesinger

ST. MARTIN'S PRESS
NEW YORK

First published in the United States by St. Martin's Press, an imprint of
St. Martin's Publishing Group

THE GREAT MONEY RESET. Copyright © 2022 by Jill Schlesinger. All rights
reserved. Printed in the United States of America. For information, address
St. Martin's Publishing Group, 120 Broadway, New York, NY 10271.

www.stmartins.com

The Library of Congress Cataloging-in-Publication Data
is available upon request.

ISBN 978-1-250-28340-5 (hardcover)

ISBN 978-1-250-28341-2 (ebook)

Our books may be purchased in bulk for promotional, educational,
or business use. Please contact your local bookseller or the
Macmillan Corporate and Premium Sales Department at 1-800-221-7945,
extension 5442, or by email at MacmillanSpecialMarkets@macmillan.com.

First Edition: 2023

10 9 8 7 6 5 4 3 2 1

For Mark,
the best Executive Producer ever,
and for the community that
we have created

Contents

Author's Note

I've written this book in hopes of giving anyone contemplating or undertaking a big life or career change the money advice they need to reach their goals. Although the people in this book are real, I've altered some names and identifying details to protect the privacy of those involved. For more discussion of key ideas covered in this book, please visit my website *Jill on Money*. Certain stories, discussions, and pieces of advice in this book first appeared there.

The
Great
Money
Reset

Introduction

Many of us fantasize about making proactive changes to our lives, whether it's reexamining a long-term relationship, telling a boss to take their job and shove it, finding a new place to live, or simply listening to a quiet, internal voice that says we must step back and figure out a new path. But relatively few of us turn those fantasies into reality. We get stuck in neutral, unable to break with our existing reality and take meaningful action.

One thirtysomething friend of mine, Melissa, escaped that trap. Since the mid-2000s she had lived on her own in New York City, working at large media companies. On a superficial level, she was happy enough. She earned a series of promotions, enjoying increasing amounts of freedom and responsibility as well as the opportunity to travel, spend time with and learn from important and interesting people, and stay in touch with current events. She also bonded with her colleagues and enjoyed their company both in and outside of the office.

Increasingly, however, Melissa wondered about her career and how it fit into her life's larger direction. The demands of her job were intense, often requiring her to work overnight hours and weekends. During one stretch, she had to show up at one o'clock in the morning for a period of months to help her team get their work done. Although she navigated the constant fatigue and managed to keep herself relatively healthy and fit, she had little time or energy left over to do what most of us do in our twenties and thirties: hang out with friends, try new hobbies and activities, and get to know who we really are. It felt like work was *all* she did.

Melissa dreamed about stepping off the fast track and doing something else that would allow her more balance and, in particular, the time and space to find a mate, maybe get married, and build a family. But again and again, she put her head down and shunted those dreams aside. Her job paid well, she was good at it, and others perceived it as interesting and glamorous. Even if she wanted to leave, a part of her doubted whether, after so long in her chosen field, she had the skills required to succeed in another career.

Melissa might have continued muddling through had the COVID-19 pandemic not shattered her long-standing status quo. As the country went into lockdown, her job, like so many others, became virtual. No longer could Melissa travel or enjoy in-person, stimulating interactions with her colleagues. It was all Zoom, all the time.

The pandemic also made her work much more complex, greatly increasing the demands on her time and worsening the stress she felt. When she wrapped up work for the day, she felt utterly exhausted—it was all she could do to turn on Netflix for a few minutes. "I found it really hard," Melissa recalled. "You've removed the happy things and things you enjoy and get fulfillment out of and you've added all of this other bullshit. And basically, I got to the point where I was working all the time and I had no life, and I was also so isolated, because I was living by myself. I kept thinking, 'This is not fun. It's not fun. It's not enough for a life.'" No amount of time binge-watching *Ted Lasso* could lift her beleaguered spirits.

With her friends and mentors telling her she was burned out, Melissa took some time off, hoping she'd return refreshed and invigorated. It didn't work out that way. Although initially she felt happy and energized to be back, the old doubts returned stronger than ever. As she now recognized, she had been so busy before the pandemic, so distracted with daily demands and the stimulation of travel and living in New York City, that she'd been able to push through month after month, year after year, without confronting her deeper doubts. "The pandemic took everything away and stripped life back to its essence. It allowed me to see very clearly that having such an intense job wasn't enough for me and that I needed to make some large-scale changes."

Checking her finances, Melissa calculated she had enough saved to allow her to take a sabbatical from work while still covering the mortgage on her condo and her other expenses. So she made a radical decision: She would quit her job and embark on an extended trip to visit friends and family across the United States.

I spoke with Melissa when she was pondering this move, and she told me that she had no job lined up upon her return and no clue what she would do. She planned to use this time away to turn off social media, detach from her day-to-day routine, get in touch with nature, take a deep look at her life, and figure out where to go from there. Would she move to a job that was less intense and remunerative but that afforded her more free time? Maybe. She'd have to see. All options were on the table, including taking a job with a different company, switching careers, even moving to a different city.

When Melissa ran the idea of quitting by her parents, they thought she was crazy. How could she leave an amazing job without another lined up? Although they did recognize the strain she'd been under, they begged her to reconsider. When she told her boss she was quitting, he also exerted pressure, doing everything possible to keep Melissa, including offering her a promotion and a sizable raise.

As tempting and flattering as that offer was, as much as she knew she'd miss her colleagues, and as scary a prospect as her impending joblessness was, Melissa went through with her decision. Her grandfather had died recently at the age of ninety-three, and at his funeral Melissa had noted the profound impact he had made on those around him. What would people say about her if she died? That she had been good at her job? Clearly that's not what she wanted.

On top of everything else, Melissa recognized that her

career, as great as it was in many respects, just didn't give her the sense of purpose she craved. Life was short, and she wanted to have a meaningful impact on those around her while she still could. It was time to take a risk and make a change.

When I heard of Melissa's frustrations and her desire to quit her job, I was deeply moved. I had gone through a major career and life transition during the late 2000s, so I empathized with the position of feeling stuck in life. I also well understood the anxiety Melissa felt at breaking with the status quo. I had been living in Providence, Rhode Island, working at a financial planning firm that I'd helped grow from a fledgling start-up to a regional powerhouse, and appearing on local radio and television on the side. After an important relationship in my life ended, I found myself asking myself the very same questions Melissa pondered.

After a period of introspection that lasted the better part of a year, I made some pivotal decisions. I moved to New York City to be with my life partner, left the financial planning field, and embarked on a new, full-time career as a business and personal finance analyst on television and radio. Although I was fortunate to have financial resources, undertaking such dramatic change all at once was scary. I was blowing up a life that in many respects was quite comfortable. What if I failed? And yet, like Melissa, I understood that our time on this earth is short and that I had to take a significant risk if I wanted to be happy.

As I pondered Melissa's story, I realized that a great many members of my radio, podcast, and television audiences were also contemplating similar transitions in their lives. Jarred by the pandemic, dozens of people wrote or spoke to me on the air about how they had begun to take a new look at their careers, lifestyles, and personal relationships. Although their specific stories differed, they all posed a question that in pre-COVID times would have seemed crazy, even impossible: Is this *really* how I want to live?

There was Gabrielle, a fifty-four-year-old office manager and bookkeeper in Ohio who, after spending fifteen months working from home due to COVID, had come to dread going back to her usual routine and wanted to know whether she had the financial wherewithal to quit her job. There was Cindy in Los Angeles, who longed for something different in her life and wondered whether she should move to the opposite coast to live for a time with her sister before perhaps taking up residence abroad. There were Cheryl and her husband, who hated the stress of big-city life and wondered if they should sell their $800,000 apartment and relocate to the small midwestern city where Cheryl's mother lived.

Still others contacted me to say that amid the upheaval of COVID they had already turned long-standing dreams into reality—and were happy to have done so. Tom emailed to report that he and his wife had sold their pricey house in Pittsburgh and moved to an Airbnb on a farm. The farm had horses (along with chickens, donkeys, and goats), which made it perfect for Tom's wife, a horseback-riding enthusiast. Without the pressure of making a sizable monthly mortgage payment or maintaining a home, Tom and his wife had more time, energy, and money to devote to their hobbies, volunteer work, and travel. Tom was ecstatic. "I would say this all came about with COVID and the time to reflect on what matters in life, which for us is family, community, and living without debt. Life is good."

Like Melissa, these audience members were usually employed and financially stable, and they had ample savings. They knew they were lucky—they would sheepishly acknowledge as much to me in describing their circumstances. But in stopping to rethink their lives, they didn't take their good fortune for granted. They wondered if the money they had accumulated would really enable them to make a big change. Could they start their own gig, transition to a new career, give back more, move clear across the country, or make a new home overseas? Could they finally create a new life for themselves after a past heartbreak, such as a divorce or the death of a loved one? Could they tell their old-school boss, "I don't really care that you want me back at the office to prove that you are a tough guy running a Very Important Business—I'm outta here"?

Those listeners like Tom, who had already made a big change, wondered something else: What would they need to do during the transitional years ahead to cope with uncertainty, consolidate their gains, and thrive?

The pandemic prompted the World Economic Forum to envision a Great Reset to the global economy, one that would address ongoing crises and improve the condition of humanity.[1] My listeners, it seemed, were poised to make a Great *Money* Reset of their own that would align their financial lives with their deepest values and desires. Forget prepandemic life, with its imperative to work like a dog, save, invest as much as possible, and contact Aunt Jill to figure out when they might retire. In the wake of COVID-19, my listeners understood that bad stuff happens, and we all must take responsibility for our happiness right now.

Perhaps you're dreaming of or already undertaking a Great Money Reset of your own. You're not alone. Millions of people are leaving their jobs either to retire early or to seek better opportunities elsewhere—as part of what media reports have termed the "Great Resignation" or the "Big Quit." Millions have uprooted themselves and their families and moved to new homes during the pandemic. But millions more of us have hesitated to take action, feeling uncertain or fearful. Some of us who have made a change have struggled, confronting challenges we might have foreseen but didn't.

It's hard to get change right, especially when it comes to our finances. To make a successful transition, we need *validation* that we're not crazy and indeed have the resources necessary to start a new chapter of our lives. We need *information* about common opportunities and traps that lie in

---

1 Klaus Schwab, "Now Is the Time for a 'Great Reset,'" World Economic Forum, June 3, 2020, https://www.weforum.org/agenda/2020/06/now-is-the-time-for-a-great-reset/.

our path and could influence our success. And most of all, we need *frameworks* for getting off our tuchuses and moving toward the life we want. Eager to make smart moves, we need solid and actionable financial advice that will help us thrive as we push our lives in bold new directions.

The Great Money Reset is your guide to getting real and building your best life. A practical handbook for navigating our present era of seismic transition, it explores ten key areas of your financial life that you must address, so that you don't look back and say to yourself, "I wish I had . . ." *The Great Money Reset* doesn't spend much time helping you pin down your personal values and priorities—there are books galore on that, not to mention qualified shrinks who can help. Instead, this book focuses on helping you move toward action once you've already done that work. It gives you the encouragement, information, and guidance required to turn your dreams and desires into positive change, in the pandemic's wake and at any transition point in your life.

I've written *The Great Money Reset* because I'm inspired by the courage it takes to listen to our emotions, honor them, and make a difficult but necessary choice. I'm inspired as well by the impulse so many people today feel to seek more meaning and fulfillment. It seems we finally are grasping money's true function and significance. We're understanding that money isn't the be-all and end-all. It's simply a tool—a critically important one, to be sure—that enables us to help others and do what enriches us spiritually and mentally. I'm writing this book because I, too, seek more meaning and purpose, and for me that means doing my part to help others along their journeys toward healthier, saner lives.

If you're pondering a Great Money Reset, or if you've already embarked on one, your path ahead might not be easy, quick, or simple. When I checked in with Melissa midway through her sabbatical, she confided that some days were extremely hard. She hadn't yet figured out what to do with the rest of her life, and she struggled with the lack of structure she now experienced without work to occupy her. "There are days," she said, "where I'm like, 'Oh my God, what did I do? This is a disaster. I gave up something so great. I threw away everything for no reason. I have no plan.'" But as time has passed, she has become more comfortable living with the ambiguity of her circumstances, and she has become aware of many parts of her old life that she doesn't miss. "I'm working on it. It's a process. I'm trying."

If you're feeling daunted by the path ahead, then I have a message for you: *You can do it.* By acting deliberately and intelligently, you can set yourself up for the greatest possible success and a happier life lived without regrets. You can take big risks and make big changes *without* jeopardizing everything you've built or consigning yourself to months of sleepless nights. You might discover that you don't even need to blow up your existing life—that a few relatively minor adjustments will suffice to make your current circumstances more meaningful and liberate you from the mental traps that have shackled you for so long.

Amid the pandemic's devastation, in which so much seems

beyond our control, we have a rare opportunity to snatch some of that control back, reaching for dreams we might have long harbored but only now dare to take seriously. Don't squander that chance. Push into it. Take bold steps to build the life you *really* want. Charge headfirst into the unknown, but for heaven's sake, do it wisely. This book shows you how.

1
Take a Good, Hard Look

If you're contemplating a big change, don't just jump into it. Stop and map out the money ramifications. This chapter shows you how to take stock of your present finances and your future needs so that you can anticipate gaps and figure out how to fill them.

In my informal discussions with listeners who either contemplated or executed a Great Money Reset, I found that the decision to shake up their lives didn't come as a sudden, seismic shift. Rather, as we saw with Melissa, most of my listeners had been moving in that direction for some time, only to find that the pandemic or some other major life event dramatically accelerated their movement and heightened their sense of urgency.

Take Ross, a caller in his mid-fifties from Texas. Ross had

built a long career in corporate America, but the last couple of years at his company had left him burned out—it's funny how three reorgs and numerous downsizing announcements will do that to a person. Ross yearned to say sayonara to the corporate world and try something completely different. His idea wasn't to quit but rather to collect his nice end-of-year bonus once more and then retire from the company. Afterward, he'd figure out his next move.

As Ross told me, he didn't harbor much ambivalence about shaking up his life. He couldn't wait to escape what he regarded as the corporate prison. But before he blew up the status quo, he did want to take a careful look at his finances.

Ross had a little less than a decade to go before his planned retirement at age sixty-five. With his wife working part-time, he was his family's primary source of income. He and his wife had three children: The older two were grown and financially independent, but their youngest was still in college and would require support for another few years. Although Ross anticipated that he would continue to work in some capacity, he likely wouldn't command the same salary he had received at his big company. Would he later come to regret his move away from corporate America, or was he secure enough moneywise to take his career in a different direction? What could he do to limit the negative financial consequences of his decision?

If you're envisioning a Great Money Reset, take a good, hard look at your finances before you leap. Most people know to do this, but their analysis often isn't rigorous or comprehensive enough. They also make the mistake of thinking they face an either-or situation: Either they make a change or they stay put. In reality, we can often make less dramatic but still satisfying moves if our finances render a wholesale change overly risky, or if the changes required to make possible our next endeavor just seem too big.

When I transitioned from working as a financial planner in quirky little Providence to an on-air financial expert in the Big Apple, my dear friend Maureen, who makes me look like a slacker when it comes to career, financial, and life planning, urged me to get a "pink notebook." This was a special journal I would use to capture my thinking and planning about my future. I would lay out my various career or life options, record any insights I gleaned while researching them, take copious notes during the many consultations I'd have with people throughout the process, and, of course, work out all of my financial plans. As I discovered, having a pink notebook was a game-changer because it kept me organized, focused, and motivated as I went through the unpredictable twists and turns of figuring out my next move.

Get yourself a pink notebook. And no, it doesn't have to be pink.

Once you have a notebook in your chosen color at hand, the question becomes how, precisely, to fill it. I won't go into all the research and exploration you might want to do if you don't quite know your future path yet and need to figure it out. But I do, of course, have a thing or two to say about the money calculations and the scenario planning that belong in any pink notebook worthy of the name.

Run Through the Fabulous Five

A proper analysis of your current financial position isn't terribly complicated. It unfolds along the lines of the financial planning process generally. I like to think about it in terms of a series of steps that I call the Fabulous Five.

Step #1: Calculate the Resources at Your Disposal (Your Current Income and Assets)

How much do you have coming in right now? If you're employed, include not just your salary but also your annual bonus and any commissions you might earn. How much savings do you currently have? Consider the full range of assets, including retirement and non-retirement accounts, your primary residence (if you own one), any investment properties you own, your emergency fund, and so on. Don't forget about the value of tax-preferenced flexible spending and dependent care accounts. Once you've tallied all of your assets, ask yourself which of them are liquid (you can convert them easily to cash without any lag time or without creating a major tax burden). When you're going through a transition, much will be unknown, and you might need more cash than you think to cover expenses you never could have predicted, to maintain a lifestyle to which you've become accustomed, or simply to provide yourself with the peace of mind that only an ample safety net can provide.

You might also need cash to cover expenses that many people neglect to consider. If you're leaving a stable, well-paying job for one that is more precarious, you might need to cover the costs of your own healthcare, life insurance, long-term disability insurance, and other benefits that your employer once subsidized. I don't think most people realize just how much health insurance costs. A healthy couple with no kids might easily spend $12,000, $15,000, or more a year on a decent plan. If you have dependent children, that number could be even greater.

People working in the public sector often have unusually generous benefits packages that they'll miss if they leave their jobs. On this basis alone, you might need more cash than you think to make a successful transition. (On the other hand, if you're in the private sector and thinking about taking a pay cut to work in a lower-stress public sector job, you might be in for a pleasant surprise. Although the pay might be lower, the value of the benefits you'll receive might make up for it.)

If you're nearing retirement, more cash on hand will allow

you to avoid tapping into retirement funds. In some situations, of course, you might well want to tap those precious funds. For example, if you plan to leave a job and greatly reduce your income, and you aren't yet ready to claim Social Security retirement benefits, it might be the ideal time to withdraw pretax retirement funds, since you'd likely be taxed at a lower bracket than you currently are now or will be in the future (more on this in Chapter 5).

During times of transition, having more cash helps us fight mounting anxiety better than a therapist, a drink, or a Klonopin ever could. Cash is the salve to the dreaded "what ifs": What if your health worsens five or ten years from now and you suddenly must shoulder greater healthcare costs or can't bring in as much income as you'd presumed? What if your new business fails? What if it takes longer than you expect to figure out your next endeavor? Stuff happens, and you want to plan for it. With cash on hand you can worry less, because you have resources at your disposal if you need them. Less worry is a good thing, right?

If many of your assets aren't liquid, and you think you could use an additional cash buffer, ask yourself whether you might be able to liquidate some of those assets—say, by selling a second home you don't use very much. But be sure to consider the tax liabilities you might face (such as capital gains) when making such decisions.

Step #2: Calculate Your Debt and Other Liabilities

How much do you currently owe? Consider the full range of debt, including mortgages, lines of credit that you have established or drawn down, credit cards, car loans, educational loans for your kids you might be paying off (didn't I tell you *not* to take on these loans in my previous book?), tax liabilities, and so on.

If you do have significant mortgage debt remaining, you might *not* want to pay that off before making a change, as you'll lose some of your precious liquidity and, in particular, money that has already been taxed. If you're in your mid-fifties, you might think that because you have $2 million in your 401(k) and a house worth $1 million with a paid-off mortgage, you're in an excellent position to retire early. Not so fast. Yes, you might not be saddled with mountains of debt, but if you don't have a strong cash reserve to draw on, you might later find yourself in a precarious position. Consider, too, that your retirement savings, once you draw on them, might not go as far as you think. If you've held these savings in traditional accounts, they haven't yet been taxed—and rest assured, they will be.

I often advise people who have even an inkling that they want to retire early or leave a well-paying job that they should start socking away non-retirement savings to the extent they can, even if it means not paying down outstanding debt as quickly.

Step #3: Consider Your Housing Situation

You've already calculated the value of your home on today's market. Think, too, about the cost of maintaining that home. In making a big change to your career, would you also want to consider downsizing your house or renting instead of owning to reduce your expenses and free up more cash? As of this writing, the real estate market is hot. If that's the case in your area, would you be missing an opportunity by not selling?

Some people, I find, become overly attached to their homes. They talk about owning a "forever home" and feel reluctant to sell it, even if doing so might make sense given their changing circumstances. Listen, nothing is forever, okay? Certainly a home isn't. Spending money now to fund that forever home—including real estate taxes, maintenance (usually about 1 to 3 percent of the value of the home annually, depending on its age and condition), utility bills, and so on—essentially means borrowing money or drawing on funds you might otherwise have saved. Month by month, you're converting liquid assets into an illiquid one. If you're someone whose life is in flux, whether because of COVID, a divorce, the death of a spouse, or some other big life change, I don't love that choice.

If you do want to stay put, check out your mortgage. If your rate is higher than prevailing rates or you have a variable, adjustable-rate, or interest-only loan, you may want to refinance it before you make big changes—remember, you might not be able to qualify once your income is reduced. You also may want to establish (but not draw down) a home equity line of credit while you still look like a good bet to the bank.

Step #4: Consider Your Spending Habits

I'll have more to say about this in a later chapter, but for now jot down your monthly expenses. How much do you currently spend on food, entertainment, transportation, clothing, and so on? Do you really need all that stuff? Do you expect your monthly expenses to decrease after you make a big change in your life, perhaps because you've moved to a city with a lower cost of living? If you're quitting your job or changing careers and expect a cut in income, are you willing to make changes to your spending habits to make your finances work?

One of the biggest mistakes people make when taking stock of their finances in preparation for a big change is to underestimate their future spending needs. It's easy to think that you could live on less than you currently do, but could you really? Will you be happy? It's best to err on the side of caution and peg your estimates closely to what you're currently spending.

Relatedly, many people nearing retirement age underestimate how long they're likely to live past retirement, and thus how much money they'll need. As a fifty-five-year-old, you might focus on the fact that you've already worked for thirty-plus years. As your trusty aunt Jill, I'm focused on the fact that you still could live for forty more years. If you plan to retire early or downshift your career, you had better make sure that your retirement savings and all other sources of income will last that long. A retirement plan that relies on your early death might work in terms of dollars and cents, but it's hardly appealing.

Step #5: Consider Obligations You Might Have to Others

Are you responsible for your kids' college expenses? What about your aging parents' nursing home expenses? Is your spouse ailing and in need of ongoing care? Is a sibling of yours perennially in financial trouble? Let's jot those down in your handy pink notebook. Consider, too, whether these expenses will likely remain stable or increase. Be conservative in your estimates. Your aging parents might be a bit more fragile physically than you think, especially in an age of COVID. With more kids in their twenties or thirties moving back home, you might have unexpected costs cropping up there as well.

Consider, too, that your priorities might be changing. Perhaps you won't want to live as far from your parents, your siblings, or your children as you once did. Perhaps you'll want to help your kids out and assume more responsibility for raising your grandchildren or funding their care. Will your kids ask you to chip in for your grandchildren's daycare or private school to make their lives easier? And if they ask, will you feel tempted to say yes? Factor all of this into your calculations.

Don't Stop at Plan A

Now that the relevant numbers are inscribed for eternity in your pink notebook, your next step is to assess the change you're thinking of making. How will it likely affect each of the Big Five over the next three years at least, and over the longer term (five years, ten years, and beyond)? Will you need to blow through a sizable portion of your assets? Will your annual income rise (thanks to a pension you might receive, for instance) or fall (because your salary will be lower or nonexistent)? Will you assume more debt or aggressively pay it down? Will your monthly living expenses including housing rise, or will you find ways to cut back? What about changes in your obligations to others?

It's usually difficult, if not impossible, to predict the future with any accuracy. That's why I strongly recommend that you plan for three different scenarios: best case, middling, and worst case. As a former pessimistic trader and supreme worrier, I usually start with worst case, but you do you.

Let's take as an example the shift I was pondering during the Great Recession: sell my home, move to a different city, embark on a new career. In a worst-case scenario, my big change would flop. I wouldn't be able to find work as an on-air media maven, covering all things financial. My girlfriend would get sick of me and throw me out on the street, causing my housing and other expenses to be double what I'd expected or more. And although my family lived in New York City, maybe I would hate living there again after a decade away and wish I'd never returned.

In a middling scenario, things would sort of work out for me. Yes, I would make a successful career transition, but the money would not be what I'd hoped, or it would take me a lot longer to make the transition, or the work would be intermittent and unpredictable. My girlfriend would decide to put up with me, but maybe we would require more space because, as you can imagine, I take up a lot of space. As a result, my housing costs might perhaps run 10 or 20 percent more than I expected. My parents or someone else in my family might suffer a health setback, requiring me to take time off from my fledgling career and limiting my earnings. I might not love my new career, but it might not be terrible, either.

In a best-case scenario, everything would work out as I'd hoped. I'd very quickly find work in the media industry making what I thought I'd make. My girlfriend and I would remain in the apartment, and I would love my new life.

Before I made my big move, I took each of these scenarios into account. Running through my numbers, I determined that my intended change was in fact realistic given my current financial situation. If the middle-case scenario came to pass, I'd also be fine moneywise with no major adjustments on my part. No, I wouldn't be thrilled working at a career that I didn't utterly love for a less-than-ideal paycheck, but I knew that I could do it and still be happy and comfortable enough for an extended period given the resources at my disposal.

If the worst-case scenario came to pass, I would activate my plan B. From my own research and experience, I knew that I could always work again as a financial planner and money manager, either joining a firm and taking a salary or going off on my own. In either case, I wouldn't be thrilled on a personal level, but I would be making a very good living. And if for some reason I couldn't find work as a financial planner, I knew that I could go always go into sales of some kind (call this plan C). Cars, software, hardware—it didn't matter, because I knew that I could sell it and make enough to support myself in New York City or elsewhere if I had to.

Sometimes Small(er) Is Better than Going Big

As I mentioned earlier, and as this analysis of my options suggests, deciding what to do with your life need not amount to an either-or choice. Almost always you can find intermediate options that might be appropriate if your best-case scenario doesn't pan out, or if your financial situation doesn't permit you to move toward your dreams all at once. Even if your financial situation is relatively strong, I invite you to consider incremental steps you might take toward achieving your dreams as you envision future scenarios.

If you hate your job and feel tempted to retire early, maybe you could make a lateral move instead, finding work in a different industry. Maybe you could move to a different firm in your present industry. Maybe you could find a different job in your current company or negotiate a different work arrangement in your current job that would allow you to fulfill at least some of your needs. If you imagine going back to school, maybe you don't have to quit and enroll full time at great expense to get your degree. Maybe you could take night classes or arrange a semester-long leave of absence from work.

If you imagine taking some time off to find yourself and figure out what would really make you happy, maybe you only take a limited time away, like a gap year (in fact, *definitely* give yourself a deadline, or you might find that a year turns into two turns into three). If a full year isn't realistic given your finances, maybe you only take six months, or three.

Each of these alternative pathways might have financial ramifications that are less extreme and more manageable than those resulting from a full-blown money reset. Incremental steps have the added benefit of allowing you to dabble in your dreams and see how you feel. Maybe incremental steps will be enough to satisfy you. Or maybe not. Melissa, from the Introduction, didn't just leap into taking six months or more off to travel and find herself. She first took a month-long leave of absence from work. Only when that didn't satisfy her did she understand that she really did need to take a bigger risk.

We often don't know what we want as well as we think we do. When Lynnda from Philadelphia left a well-paying but demanding job in sales in 2019, she was eager to pursue her long-standing dream of working full-time as an actress. She had done some acting in her twenties and now, at age sixty-six, was prepared to put it all out there again. Auditioning for several roles in theatrical productions, she discovered that directors weren't eager to hire someone who had taken a forty-year hiatus from the profession. Even more interesting, she didn't really like the theater as much as she imagined she would. "I guess the dream changed," she said.

Lynnda wound up auditioning to record audio books. In March 2020, she got her first assignment. Eighteen months later, she had recorded twenty-three books across genres. "It's been a blast!" she said in an email. "I'm not a person who can *not* work, so this is perfect for me. I get to utilize my creativity, I've learned some audio engineering skills, and I'm reading fun, interesting books! Love that!" Your plans might take you in wonderful (and not-so-wonderful) directions that you can't predict right now. Before you go all in, taking some smaller steps first might serve you well.

Jamal, a thirty-two-year-old from Portland, Oregon, discovered that he had become the go-to guy at his sports apparel company during the annual open enrollment period for benefits. Word got around that he wasn't just "Jamal in tech" but the guy who was building spreadsheets to help his co-workers find the most affordable health plan and the least expensive investment options within the firm's 401(k). When the pandemic hit, he helped some of his co-workers who were downsized roll over their retirement plans, and he also became somewhat of a lay expert in navigating COBRA.

"I was basically becoming the in-house financial planner to my friends and colleagues," he told me, "so I started to investigate what it would mean to actually become a Certified Financial Planner."

Learning that the process can take a few years, he decided he wasn't ready to chuck a career at his present company just yet. So he committed to completing the coursework to sit for the CFP exam and began researching which firms in his area would let him intern while he remained employed. "Look, I still have student loans, so I can't bail on this job until I get my own financial house in order, but at least I have a plan of action that could help me one day become a full-time financial planner." Jamal had found a middle ground, one that would allow him to move ahead without unduly disrupting his present life or forcing him to assume too much risk.

In contemplating and experimenting with less dramatic steps, consider what you *really* are seeking out of a change. If you dream of quitting your job, do you want to quit, or is your current boss the real problem? In the latter case, you might not need to quit—simply transferring to another job elsewhere in your organization could do the trick. If you imagine leaving your city and moving out of state, maybe you don't have to make such a big move. Thinking about why the move sounds so appealing to you, maybe you'll find that it isn't the change of scenery per se that you crave, but simply the chance to live more cheaply. If that's the case, moving to a cheaper suburb a half hour away might serve as a good substitute, or at least an interim step toward something bigger.

I beg you to ask these kinds of questions of yourself repeatedly, and to ask trusted friends, relatives, and counselors what they think as well. In many cases, our gripes about the present and our dreams about the future rest on hidden assumptions we're making that might not bear out. It would be a shame—and perhaps pose a serious problem—if we wound up blowing up our careers or our lives to solve a problem that didn't exist. Before you rush to take action, making decisions you can't easily reverse, home in on the real problem and solve for that.

When you think of backup plans to go with your various scenarios (best-case, middle-case, worst-case), don't just sketch them out. Do the legwork to put those plans in place so they're there if you need them. I didn't just say, "Oh, I'll go back to financial planning if a career in media doesn't work out." I contacted a friend of mine who owned a financial planning and investment management firm, told him of my plans, and asked if I might come to work for him if media didn't work out for me. To my delight, he told me that I always had a job if I ever needed one. Do you think that took some of the pressure off? Abso-friggin'-lutely.

If you're married or otherwise partnered, there's an additional wrinkle to consider when running through the Fabulous Five and envisioning specific scenarios. What can your spouse or partner tolerate? You might be able to swallow making 50 percent a year less than you currently do, or slashing your discretionary spending by a thousand dollars a month to make the numbers work, or taking retirement at age sixty-eight instead of age sixty-two, but does your significant other feel similarly? If not, you might be in for some trouble (such as an unforeseen and unwanted change in your relationship status) if you go ahead with a big move.

When I moved to New York, I initially landed a salaried job with CBS, even though I dreamed of working for myself. A few years later, when I had a chance to do similar work in media but operate as a freelancer, I jumped at it. Knowing that the lack of guaranteed income might stress out my partner, I promised her that no matter what happened, I would pull in at least a certain minimum income as a freelancer. If I couldn't, I would reconsider that choice. This helped her feel good about my shift to working for myself. Happily, I've always been able (knock on wood) to live up to my end of the bargain. It hasn't hurt that she's achieved more financial stability in her career as well.

So far, I haven't said much about an obvious option available to you: staying precisely where you are and gutting it out for a while longer. I want to encourage you to move toward your dreams and to battle the forces of fear and inertia that might hold you back. But in some circumstances, staying put and gutting it out is in fact the best answer. If you only have three more years to work before you'll be eligible for a nice, juicy pension, then make the responsible choice and stay—don't be a child. Of course, if staying a minute longer will result in a nervous breakdown or worse, then yes, leaving would be the more responsible choice.

When we're contemplating big moves in our lives, we're often in a place of heightened emotion, frustrated as we are with the status quo. One of the best reasons to crack open a pink notebook and take stock of your finances is precisely to give your emotions a chance to cool. When you do, you might find that a change is the *opposite* of what you want.

During the first year of the pandemic, a good friend of mine came very close to ending a twenty-five-year relationship. She had worked herself into a tizzy, convincing herself that she hated being coupled and that the right answer was to take up with a woman ten years younger. When I reminded her that COVID was happening and nobody was happy, she assured me that her discontent was real: "I'm great friends with my wife, but our sex life is nonexistent. I'm fifty years old. Life is passing me by. The pandemic is making me feel like anything can happen, so why am I staying in this place?"

She didn't start a pink notebook—at least not that I'm aware of—but she did step back and consider the financial consequences of divorce at her age. She also, to her credit, went into serious therapy and convinced her wife to begin marriage counseling. In the end, she decided that even if their sex life would never meet her expectations, she did love her wife and would find the most happiness if she stayed. So she did.

Bottom line: Don't be afraid to blow things up. But please, don't do it if you don't have to—or if you shouldn't.

The Power of Taking Stock

When Ross from Texas told me he had a hankering to leave his dumb old corporate job but wanted help thinking it through, I was more than happy to oblige. We ran through many of the basics. I learned that he earned $150,000 a year base salary, with an extra $25,000 bonus. His wife pulled in about $10,000–$20,000 a year working part-time. The couple had about $2 million in retirement savings, with $1.8 million of that in a 401(k). They also owned an investment property worth $237,000 with a large outstanding mortgage balance but a positive cash flow of $600 a month.

Ross and his wife owned a primary residence valued at about $580,000 that was almost paid off—just another $55,000 to go—and they planned to stay in that house if he left corporate America. Finally, they had amassed a decent-sized emergency fund of $65,000.

As we considered future scenarios, Ross told me he anticipated he'd need about $80,000 to $90,000 in post-tax retirement income to maintain their desired standard of living. If he waited until age seventy to claim his pension, he would receive $500 a month. If he wanted to claim it early as a lump sum, he would receive $90,000. If Ross and his wife waited until age seventy to claim Social Security retirement benefits, they could count on a combined $57,000 a year in income from that. Ross said that he didn't want to touch his retirement savings until starting to draw on it at age sixty-five—almost a decade from now—if he could help it.

As I worked through Ross's situation with him, I found myself getting a little nervous about his open-ended plan to leave his corporate job without a clear plan for bringing in income. The decade between now and age sixty-five was a critical time. With his wife continuing to work part-time, he would need to bring in over $100,000 each year pre-tax to cover his expenses if he didn't want to tap into his savings. He also would need to figure out a way to cover his and his wife's health insurance costs.

Retiring outright would be a bold move—probably too bold. Even quitting his current position to work at a low-paying job or to work part-time would expose Ross and his family to too much risk. I asked Ross if he thought he could find a job similar to his current one that he would enjoy more and that would allow him to earn a six-figure salary. He said he thought he could. He also related that his current company would cover his medical insurance for another five years once he left, a benefit that would afford him more flexibility.

Overall, I thought Ross would be best served by doing not a total Money Reset but a partial one. Yes, he could eventually leave his corporate job, telling his company and his boss to take a hike. But he shouldn't just go out and get an entry-level job afterward or embark on a risky start-up venture that would require taking a low base pay for the promise of a future payoff. His best move was to use his existing skill set to obtain another stable, reasonably well-paying job that he found more palatable and finish out his working career for another decade or so. If he could dedicate himself to this middle road, he'd address his current job frustrations in the short term *and* likely enjoy a more comfortable and less stressful retirement later on.

Take the time to run the numbers, and you, too, might find that those dreams of making a change are more realistic than you think. Maybe you have the financial resources in place to live those dreams exactly as you imagine them. Or maybe prudence will dictate that you tone down those dreams a bit while still getting most of what you want. Maybe the knowledge that you could make a change is all you really needed in the first place. I used to call this "plan F," as in I could tell my boss to f— off at any time and know that I would be just fine. Regardless, taking stock of your financial life gives you more control, allowing you to take smarter, more thoughtful, and perhaps more nuanced risks.

If you do decide to take action, or even if you don't, mapping out your money can leave you more confident in the soundness of your choice. Since others in your life might be offering their (sometimes unsolicited and conflicting) advice, performing an analysis allows you to cut through any confusion you might be experiencing and to feel empowered. Ross now *knows* he can afford to leave his job with the caveats just mentioned. As described in the Introduction, Melissa *knew* she could take the big (for her) step of quitting and putting her career on pause for the first time in fifteen years, because she had run the numbers. When her parents confronted her with their doubts, she had actual data to reassure them—and herself.

Many of us somehow feel we lack permission to make a change. I hereby grant you that permission, on one condition: Get your numbers straight. I don't know if a Great Money Reset, or some lesser version of one, is right for you. But you don't know it, either, unless you stop dreaming for a moment, sit your butt down, and do the math.

Rock the Reset

- Take an honest look at your finances before you leap.

- Focus your analysis on the Fabulous Five: resources, liabilities, housing situation, spending, outstanding obligations.

- Create best-case, middling, and worst-case scenarios for the future, and consider taking incremental steps rather than a single, big leap.

2

Curb Your Consumption

You might think you must blow your life savings to make a big change. Maybe not. People from all walks of life are rethinking their consumption habits. You can do the same, with an eye toward reducing expenses and directing those resources toward your dreams. If you spent a bit more frugally earlier in life, then congratulations—your payoff awaits, but only if you're willing to let go of your inner Scrooge.

There's a powerful secret to achieving your dreams that I've been applying for some time, with considerable success. For the price of this book, I'm happy to let you in on it. It's a behavioral strategy that's simple, easy to apply, and guaranteed to work. Anyone can use it to feel more empowered financially, irrespective of where they live, how much they earn, or what they do for a living. So, are you ready? The secret to achieving your dreams is . . . *spend less*.

I know, brilliant, right? But as my listener Julie from Salt Lake City recently reminded me, it really does work. Julie didn't always live in the majestic Beehive State, home to spectacular views, a wonderful climate, a dynamic culture, and endless outdoor leisure opportunities. For many years she lived in cold, dreary Boston, making around $40,000 a year working as a lab technician at a big university. She was married at the time, and her husband earned a similar amount working as a sound engineer in a recording studio.

In late 2019, just before the pandemic, Julie's employer made her an enticing early retirement offer. She was sixty-one years old and recently divorced. If she agreed to retire, her university would pay her a year's salary as severance. And it would also cover the cost of her health insurance for the rest of her life. Not bad!

Julie jumped at the offer. She had always loved Salt Lake City and dreamed of moving there in retirement. Now she could do it a full *nine years earlier* than expected (she had planned on retiring at age seventy), while she was still feeling young and vigorous. In March 2020, she sold her house, which she owned outright, pocketing $500,000. She sold her antiques collection, packed up her other stuff, looked for apartments in Salt Lake City over Zoom, and in a matter of weeks relocated there.

When I first heard of Julie's precipitous move, I wondered whether it was such a good idea. Julie wasn't sitting on piles of cash. Besides the half million in house proceeds, she had a modest amount in savings, in the tens of thousands of dollars. I doubted she would be able to live a reasonable lifestyle without running out of money in retirement.

Julie begged to differ. Having run an analysis of her current financial position similar to the one in Chapter 1, she concluded that if she took the university's offer, sold her house, and continued to work part-time, she could cover her monthly expenses of $2,500 before claiming Social Security retirement benefits at age seventy. After that point, her monthly government check and interest from her nest egg would continue to fund her active lifestyle.

The key here was her expenses. To some, $2,500 might sound like a lot, but it really isn't. When you consider that the average rent in Salt Lake City as of this writing in 2021 was about $1,200 and rising, and that Julie would also have to pay for utilities, transportation, food, entertainment, and any extras out of her remaining budget, her plan seemed overly aggressive to me. I put it to Julie: Would she really be able to subsist on $2,500 a month without feeling as if she were living like a pauper? Even if she could do so at first, how long would it take for her to either start busting through her monthly budget or become mired in depression because she was sticking to it?

In response, Julie said something that really surprised me: "But Jill, I've been living on $2,500 all along."

No way—in pricey Boston?

Yes. Julie hadn't earned a high salary over the years, but she always had been careful with her money. Each month, she and her former husband had set aside funds for four regular expenses: homeowner's insurance, property tax, auto insurance, and flood insurance. Any additional spending, such as eating out or buying new clothes, came after they'd accounted for those items as well as their rent (and, later, their mortgage payment). Julie also made sure to stash a bit of cash away every month in savings.

Julie and her husband hadn't indulged excessively, but Julie assured me they hadn't lived like monks. Theirs was a fun but measured life. They went out to eat occasionally but not every week. They traveled but didn't book first-class accommodations. "I know how to spend," Julie told me. "I can buy a beautiful bag if I want to do that. But I choose not to. I can take a big, expensive trip, but I make it work by living frugally for ten months. Overall, I've never felt like I've lived in deprivation."

Most people I meet think they must slash their spending habits dramatically to live in retirement without a regular paycheck. Julie didn't have to do that—and with her employer's offer, she was also well positioned to retire early, without debt and with modest savings—because she had adopted smart, thoughtful consumption habits all along. As Julie insists, most of us can achieve our financial dreams if we simply muster a bit of discipline around spending. "You have to know you can do this. You must have a savings mindset and be responsible to yourself. You'll find out that you don't need the stuff that you think you need."

It's always a good time to keep closer track of your spending and to put a plan in place to spend below your means. But it's especially important to do so if you're thinking of embarking on a significant transition in your life. Even if you haven't always been as disciplined with your wallet as Julie, you might still be able to make a money reset work by exerting more control over your spending.

If you expect you'll need $10,000 a month in retirement, perhaps you only need $8,000—a difference that might allow you to push forward your retirement age by several years. Or let's say you want to move to a different city but don't see how you can afford it. A careful look at your spending might reveal that it's possible—because with a little discipline and creativity you'd probably be able to live well on $4,000 per month rather than the $5,000 you're spending today.

We all know that spending matters, but most of us don't really stop to analyze it. Disciplining ourselves to scrimp and save isn't sexy, and keeping track of where our money goes each month can be a pain in the tush. But without a clear picture, we fall into irrational and mindless habits that drain our finances without enhancing our happiness. Let's break these habits. Let's gain a deeper understanding of *why* we buy what we buy and whether it really serves us. Gaining more control over our spending really can give us more flexibility and freedom to act. And among us financial planner types, that *is* pretty sexy.

The Great Consumer Rethink

You've probably already started to review your consumption habits—I know I have. The pandemic prompted a wholesale rethinking of purchase behavior across America. Almost overnight, people parted with habits they'd kept in place for years, even decades. They stopped going to the grocery store and relied on delivery services instead. They stopped going to the movies and attending concerts and said hello to Netflix. They stopped going to the gym and bought themselves a Peloton, took power walks, or played pickleball with friends. They stopped traveling and took up hobbies like gardening or baking bread.

Consumers didn't simply seek substitutes for their previous purchases—for instance, by venturing from brick-and-mortar stores to online. They also questioned whether longtime spending patterns were necessary at all. In many cases, they liberated themselves from purchases they had never before thought to question—outlays that were gobbling up their discretionary funds without adding much lasting value.

Thanks to the pandemic, I could finally say adios to a work-induced fashion addiction that had been building up—and filling up my closets—for years. Let me be clear: I'm not all that into fashion and shopping. I do like nice things, but mainly I've spent thousands of dollars each year (I can't and won't divulge the exact number) on my appearance, including shoes, clothes, hair, and makeup, because I thought I needed to promote a certain image for my television appearances. I told myself that people cared about what I looked like (TV is a visual medium, after all), so I had to keep my wardrobe current and my look top-notch.

When the pandemic arrived, I stopped worrying about being the snazziest dresser that ever graced the small screen. As I now saw it, this wasn't part of my job description. Rather, I was the money expert who came in to make economic and financial topics relevant, comprehensible, and dare I say entertaining for millions of viewers, then went on her merry way. Why did I have to spend $750 on a pair of new shoes that people might see for seven seconds and barely notice?

I still have a fashion budget, but my expenditures today are only about a quarter of what they once were. I'm able to take that savings and channel it in ways that are more meaningful to me—like paying more to the people who work with me and investing in the technology that enables me to work more efficiently. Do I miss doing all that extra and unnecessary shopping? Heck, no. And my partner is relieved that she now has a little more space to store her shoes!

In many cases, the pandemic prompted us to question our spending because we *couldn't* consume in ways that we were used to. Did we really miss going out to restaurants, say, or going to the theater? I know I did, so as the pandemic eased, I began to consume in those areas again. But I didn't miss traveling nearly as much as I expected, and don't even get me started on business travel. Will I continue to do that? Yes, if the right opportunities arise. But like many professionals,

I'm not rushing to travel multiple times a month on business. Now that I've experienced what it's like *not* to feel the constant stress of packing my bags, racing to the airport, scrunching myself into a seat for hours on end, sleeping in an unfamiliar hotel bed at night, and being away from my beloved puppies, I don't want to go back.

We'll all come to different conclusions on these points. Some women I know have sworn off regular mani-pedis since the pandemic. They realize that these services were expensive, and they just didn't get that much out of them. Other women missed their regular grooming appointments immensely, as it was their one chance during the week to leave their kids at home and enjoy some "me time." Who is right? All of them. Rather than arriving at ironclad judgments about any particular consumption choice, it's most helpful simply to become more mindful of how we're spending our hard-earned money and how it makes *us* feel.

When making a big move in your life, you could benefit from taking this kind of background reflection to the next level. Methodically observe your full range of experience as a consumer and ponder it. Look at yourself as an anthropologist might, with detached scientific interest, and ask yourself: What am I really doing here? And why? What might I do differently? How much could I save? And where might I channel that money to better serve my needs and desires?

One way to approach this kind of analysis is to run through the various dimensions of your discretionary consumption individually—food, entertainment, travel, media, clothing, and so on—and map out your habits. But I've got another way that might be even better.

Examine Your Spending Rules

Drazen Prelec, a professor at MIT, studies the complex psychology that underlies our buying behavior, particularly irrational choices we might make. As he observes, people tend to deploy a jungle-gym-like accumulation of rules when they consume, giving our spending a moral tinge. We might tell ourselves that we'll never wear a particular brand because it's too expensive. (One television anchor called me out and said, "I know that you are wearing Akris—I just can't bite the bullet and spend that kind of money!") We might proclaim that we'll only eat out once a week, or that we'll avoid a super-expensive cut of meat. Sometimes we stick to these self-imposed and often sensible rules, but other times we don't, and then we feel bad about it.[1]

This dynamic strongly resembles how many of us behave when we diet. With the best of intentions, we define rules about which foods and how much of them we can eat or how much alcohol we can drink. Then a Saturday night out with friends comes along, and our rules go out the window. Afterward

---

1 Eve Downing, "The Psychology of Spending," *MIT Spectrum*, Winter 1999, https://spectrum.mit.edu/winter-1999/the-psychology-of-spending/.

we feel terrible and resolve to stick even more tightly to the rules, going forward.

To engage in healthy practices regarding money, it helps to become more aware of what these rules of ours are at any given point in time. The rules are often subtle, unspoken, and hidden to us. We take them for granted, often having adopted them from our parents, friends, or culture. As we catalogue our rules, we must ask: Do they really serve us well, helping us to gain a sense of control and contributing to our overall happiness? Or do they trap us, leading us to spend in unhelpful ways and dooming us to a perpetual struggle that saps our self-confidence?

Uncovering our spending rules isn't straightforward—it leads us into the complex netherworld that is our emotions. Here are some questions I recommend asking to help you understand your consumer behavior and the underlying psychology as completely as possible.

Question #1: What Do I Really Need in My Life, and What Do I Only Think I Need?

Many of us create rules premised on the idea that we require certain goods or services to be happy and healthy. We all must make purchases corresponding to the lower rungs of the psychologist Abraham Maslow's famous hierarchy of needs— food, water, a safe place to live, heat, healthcare, and so on. When it comes to higher-order needs such as our need to feel connected to others or our need to be creative and feel self-actualized, our required purchases become less obvious. Do we tell ourselves we must belong to a country club to feel a sense of belonging and connection with others? That's a rule we make up for ourselves. Might there be some other way to feel connected that doesn't involve paying thousands of dollars or more a year for the right to play golf and eat subpar (excuse the pun, golfers!) food in the dining room? Perhaps so.

We might think it necessary to send our kids to private school in order to feel a sense of value and self-worth as a parent. That's another mental rule. But is it helping us? Or are we spending tens of thousands of dollars a year for an educational opportunity that doesn't really add much value to our family, simply because we've come to make certain assumptions about private and public schools, our parental obligations, and what's best for our children? We might think we need to live in a 3,500-square-foot house to be happy. But now that our kids are out of the house, should that rule still apply?

Even our most basic needs might not require spending in the short term depending on the circumstances. During the early part of the pandemic, someone asked me on the air to help them prioritize which bills to pay. You might presume that your mortgage and utility bills would rank high on the list, and ordinarily they would. But as I explained, banks and utility companies would likely cut people some slack in paying those bills if they lost their jobs due to the total economic shutdown associated with COVID-19. So the rule in our heads telling us that we must absolutely, positively pay our mortgage bill every month no matter what temporarily didn't apply. We could direct our scarce resources to other important, short-term needs, like buying food and vital medicines.

Prior to the pandemic, I devoted time and energy to promoting an important rule that I called "The Big Three." (Shameless plug: You might remember this from my first book, *The Dumb Things Smart People Do with Their Money*.) Regardless of your station in life, when setting financial goals, I argued, you should focus on establishing emergency reserve funds, paying down consumer debt, and funneling as much money as possible into your retirement savings. I gave mostly equal weight to each priority, depending on the situation. During the pandemic, I modified this rule. What mattered most, and what probably still matters in our volatile age, is to bolster our emergency funds. We never know when the next crisis will arise, whether it's a global pandemic, a job loss, or a personal health crisis, and we must ensure that we have sufficient cash at our disposal.

If you're completely out of touch with your monthly spending, charting the rules in your head that relate to your basic needs is a great place to start. Figure out what your true absolutes in life are, and whether any apparent needs on your list are really desires. This shouldn't be all that hard, considering that starting in March 2020 we got a crash course in what's important. Consider as well if any cheaper options exist that would allow you to fulfill your needs. You might decide that the public schools are so bad in your area that private school really is a need—that rule of yours holds up.

But must you send your child to the most expensive private school, or might a cheaper one be perfectly acceptable? Yes, food is a necessity, but must all of your produce be organic (a rule that many of us adopt), or can you go for cheaper, conventional options for certain fruits and vegetables? Needs are sometimes not what we think. And the rules we follow in this area might be long overdue for revision.

Question #2: Do I Ever Find Myself Feeling Guilty, Insecure, or Anxious About a Purchase I Make?

We all hate to feel bad about our spending, but all too often we do. Analyzing these occasions can help tease out unspoken rules. Do we feel compelled to get others' validation before we make a big purchase? Why might that be? Are we making purchases without trusting what our gut says, or even in direct contravention of what we know to be good for us? Perhaps we should revisit those purchasing choices and the assumptions that underlie them. Are our friends or family members unduly influencing our spending? What values of theirs have infiltrated our thinking when it comes to money?

Posing these questions, we might come to find, for instance, that we are spending hundreds of dollars going out each weekend night with our friends, not because we really want or need those social experiences, but because our friends party like rock stars and we feel pressure to conform. What would happen if we overcame our FOMO and broke the "I must go out every Friday or Saturday night or I'm lame" rule? Maybe we'd *enjoy* staying in once a week, and if our friends didn't get that, maybe we'd find ourselves gravitating toward a new set of friends. All the money we'd save staying in might unlock more opportunity for us, making the difference between being able to undertake a big money reset move or languishing in our present, not-so-great state.

It's so easy to allow others to influence our spending. We also might find that one spending decision we make leads to others that, in the back of our minds, we know aren't necessarily good for us. If we're paying for expensive private school for our kids on a relatively modest salary, we might also find ourselves drawn into paying for fancy soccer camp or private math tutoring or splurging on extravagant holiday gifts because everyone else in our kids' school is doing that. Learn to listen to those nagging doubts you have around spending and to question the rules you're following that give rise to them.

Anxiety is an especially important emotion to consider in regard to our spending—and a definite red flag. A man I know, Bert, is fifty years old and single. He was married once and after his divorce decided that he'd never get into another long-term relationship. As luck would have it, he did exactly that, becoming serious with a wealthy woman who tended to spend extravagantly. Bert is no pauper—he has $5 million to his name. But as he told me, "I find myself spending so much money to just keep pace with her lifestyle that it's freaking me out."

We're not talking here about splurging on a moderately luxurious vacation—Bert could handle that. But this woman was used to flying on private jets and inviting a whole posse of friends and family members to come along. An unspoken rule was at play in Bert's mind that desperately needed examining: "It's okay for me to spend whatever it takes for the sake of this relationship that I enjoy, even if it wigs me out a little." The factor that prodded Bert to review this rule was the mounting anxiety he felt, fed, of course, by calls from his worried financial advisor that he was spending way too much.

Question #3: Do I Find Myself Making Impulsive Purchases? If So, When and Why?

All of us spend impulsively on occasion, and thinking about when, why, and how we do this can clue us in to underlying emotions that might be fueling our spending. We might find that we're spending to distract ourselves from fear or sadness. A close friend or family member is sick, for instance, and to get our mind off the sadness or pain we feel, we go into a Nordstrom and drop some cash on an unneeded Burberry sweater. Or perhaps we're spending because we're stressed. We're so overwhelmed at work that we impulsively decide we'll go out for dinner, just to have a chance to relax and feel pampered. We also might order a more expensive meal—that $60 steak—because the act of indulging gives us a hit of dopamine and eases our stress.

Impulse purchases don't always translate into spending rules, but sometimes they do. We might find that we're allowing ourselves to splurge at an expensive restaurant twice a month, even though it's a big drain on our discretionary income, because we're stressed and feel we deserve it. That's a rule: "I'm allowed to indulge twice a month on food." Is it a good rule, given our current life and financial goals? Or might there be other, equally effective ways to deal with the underlying stress that don't result in a bloated monthly credit card bill and allow us to channel our resources more productively?

Question #4: Are Relationship Dynamics Influencing My Spending?

If you're in a relationship, paying attention to how you and your partner engage around money is extremely important. Do you make money decisions together? If so, how, exactly? Do you frequently disagree and make compromises to keep the peace? Does one or the other of you earn more and thus exercise more sway over financial matters? Do you tend to divide and conquer when it comes to money, with one of you handling certain bills and spending decisions to the exclusion of the other, and vice versa?

Paying attention to tensions when they arise can help you surface hidden spending rules. Kelly, a respected artist, recently got engaged on her fiftieth birthday. A brush with mortality had led her to push for a wedding with her long-term boyfriend. As she put it to me, "Nobody's promising you tomorrow. So what are we doing today?" Her boyfriend agreed to get married, but he argued that if they did, they should get their act together and finally buy a house.

The notion of being a homeowner freaked Kelly out. When she was a child, her dad lost his job soon after her family bought a house. The resulting hardships traumatized her, making it very difficult for her to spend money on herself as an adult, even when the spending was reasonable and would increase her happiness. A series of highly restrictive rules popped into her head around spending—what was permissible, what wasn't. Her boyfriend was able to help her see that spending a relatively modest sum on a house, given their incomes, was perfectly fine and need not cause her any stress.

Pondering how you and your partner jointly handle money can reveal additional rules that shape your spending. Perhaps one or the other of you feels strange spending money on certain kinds of goods and services because of your upbringing. Or perhaps the two of you arrive at certain spending rules to reduce anxieties that one or the other of you feels. Decide together whether these rules are necessary and if they're helping you to achieve your dreams or holding you back. How might you adjust your spending to save money while still keeping both of you reasonably sane and happy?

When In Doubt, Run an Experiment

In posing these questions and identifying and assessing your rules, make sure that you ask enough follow-up questions, as these will generally lead to the best, most interesting insights and possibilities. Take a person who believes they must continue living in their 3,500-square-foot house after they've become an empty-nester. That person might say, "Well, I actually do need that space, because I need a place for the kids to stay when they come home for the holidays." Fine. But then ask another question: "How often each year will all of my kids really come home at once and require a place to stay?"

If the answer is only once or twice per year, the next question might be: "Could you think of some alternative way to be together on those occasions—for instance, by getting the kids hotel rooms nearby or spending these big family holidays away at a resort?" If the answer to that question is no, then further inquiry might turn up some deeper emotional concerns that are shaping this person's spending decisions. If they don't ask these questions, they'll never be able to pin down their needs and desires with precision. They'll also never be able to understand what they'll truly require to satisfy them and where unexpected savings might be possible.

As you unearth important spending rules, consider how the big changes you're thinking of making will affect you. If some of your rules originate because you're trying to deal with stress, will moving to a new city, taking a new job, proposing to a romantic partner, or making some other change alleviate that stress or add to it? Will you be moving away from friends or family who have influenced your spending, allowing you to change some of your unspoken rules? If you're struggling to make an intended change work financially, how might you realistically adjust your spending to improve your financial situation? Which of your current rules are susceptible to change and which aren't?

You can think all of this through, but sometimes it's best to frame a hypothesis about potential spending adjustments and run an experiment. A friend of mine in his early thirties, Blair, was bored to tears by his corporate job in brand marketing. He earned most of the money in his household, about $140,000 per year (I know, not bad for a guy so early in his career). His husband, Mitchell, was a public school teacher whose job provided great benefits but relatively low pay.

As part of his job, Blair helped to launch a podcast, and he found that he loved it. He dreamed of shelving his marketing career and becoming a podcast producer full-time. Jobs were plentiful in this area, but in the best-case scenario, Blair would probably only earn $70,000 as a podcast producer, half his former salary. Would the couple be able to manage without making unacceptable changes to their lifestyle?

Scrutinizing their spending, Blair suspected that they could make their finances work if they left their current rental apartment and found a cheaper one in a different neighborhood, and if they cut back significantly on their spending. Blair felt uncomfortable making the leap all at once, so he decided to run a short-term experiment. The couple would stay in their current apartment, but for a period of several months they would try to live on $70,000 less than they had been doing.

Practically speaking, that would mean thoroughly revisiting their spending decisions—every dinner out, every vacation, every nonessential fashion expenditure, and so on. Mitchell was up for it: He didn't like seeing Blair unhappy with his job, and he wanted to devise a solution. It helped that the pandemic was under way, causing the couple to naturally cut back on a great deal of nonessential spending. As the country began to open back up, the couple decided to stick to some of their pandemic-era frugality, continuing to cook more, stay in more often, and forgo weekend getaways.

Blair and Mitchell had never reviewed their spending before—they'd simply bought whatever they wanted. Now they realized that they had been buying goods, services, and experiences that they didn't need, especially if Blair had to make himself miserable at work to fund them. With further introspection, it became clear that they spent some of this money in part to help distract him from all the dissatisfaction and stress he felt at work. In other words, their mindless spending had helped keep Blair tethered to a job he disliked. Once they began making do with less, they were amazed at how much they were saving—about $50,000 in a little over a year.

When I spoke with Blair, the couple had decided to make some big changes. Blair was still in his job, but he was looking for a new one, and the couple was searching for a new apartment in a neighborhood that was not "hip" but that afforded some cheaper options. In the meantime, they were keeping their revamped spending rules in place and continuing to save. Their growing nest egg would only open more possibilities as the two decided which new job Blair would take and which new apartment they would rent.

Blair and Mitchell's experience echoes Julie's from earlier in the chapter. Chances are, we don't need so much *stuff* in our lives. But it is possible to cut back too much on spending, to the point where it isn't sustainable. To avoid that scenario, we might all benefit from going slowly and experimenting to see how reductions or other shifts in spending really feel. Maybe we won't mind them. Maybe we will. Either way, it's important to know.

Keep It Real

To round out this chapter, let me tell you one more story that's worth pondering. Marjorie and Brent are in their early fifties, the parents of two middle-schoolers. Brent earned about $100,000 and was self-employed, while Marjorie brought home $125,000 a year as a marketing executive. During the pandemic, Marjorie's firm unexpectedly laid her off. For about a year, she stayed at home with the kids, and the family lived on Brent's income. As the pandemic eased, Marjorie was considering whether to go back to work. As she discovered, she really didn't want to.

Marjorie called me because she was thinking of opting out of the workforce for good and wanted to make sure she could do that without sacrificing the couple's goals of paying for their kids' college educations and retiring in relative comfort. Marjorie felt confident that it was possible. As she pointed out, she and her husband had managed to amass $800,000 in retirement savings. Their house was worth $750,000 and only $250,000 remained on their mortgage. By reining in their spending, the family had grown accustomed to living on Brent's income alone, which had remained unchanged. What was keeping her from bowing out of the workforce and continuing to enjoy a more relaxed life at home?

Running through the numbers, I concluded that Marjorie was deluding herself, big-time. The couple had no emergency fund—a major Aunt Jill no-no. They had no money socked away for their kids' educations, and little prospect of saving more on Brent's income alone. As for retirement, forget about it. Sure, the $800,000 would continue to grow over the next decade or more, but on one salary, they wouldn't be able to save any more going forward. In addition, they would have to pay for their own health insurance, since Brent was self-employed.

If Marjorie and Brent wanted to sell their home and sock away the $500,000 in equity, and if they were willing to slash their expenses even more dramatically by moving to a much cheaper locale, then maybe—*maybe*—Marjorie could continue to stay home. I also wondered if Marjorie might consider ending her career but taking a part-time job. If she worked at a large chain like Starbucks, for instance, she could ease the stresses she had felt at her corporate job, bring home hundreds of dollars a week, and obtain health insurance. Taking that step would allow the couple to save at least something for retirement and their children's education.

It wasn't clear that Marjorie had an appetite to work part-time or sell the family home. In that case, she was stuck in a bind: sacrifice the family's financial goals or go back to work full-time. I'm not sure what she'll decide, but her quandary holds a lesson for the rest of us. As important as it is to review our spending and pare it back, it might not be enough by itself to enable a major money reset. To maximize your opportunities for future growth and change, the best approach is ultimately the one that Julie lived by and that many of us struggle to adopt: Understand your spending and keep it in check all along. That way, when you experience the urge to shake up your life, you'll have what you need.

Rock the Reset

- The not-so-hidden secret to achieving your dreams is: *spend less.*
- Question what you need, whether purchases you make cause you to feel bad, whether you make impulsive purchases, and whether relationships influence your spending.
- Experiment with significant changes to your spending to see if they will stick.

3

Bully Your Boss

My, how the tables have turned. After two decades during which employers held all the cards in the labor market, many workers have finally obtained an advantage. In this chapter, we explore how to parlay a newfound bargaining position into the exciting life you want. Even in tighter labor markets, knowing how to bully your boss remains an essential career skill. As my mom likes to say, "If you don't ask, you don't get."

Arun was in his late twenties, making $75,000 a year at a job in social media marketing. That had sounded like a pretty good salary when he took the job five years ago, but as he since discovered, in a large, pricey metropolitan area like his, it really wasn't. Each month, Arun forked over an exorbitant sum for the privilege of living with two roommates in a smelly, overheated, roach-infested apartment. Factor in food, health insurance, and payments on his college loans, and Arun had very little left over each month for savings.

As bad as his financial situation was, Arun stuck it out without receiving the promotion and raise he felt he deserved because he otherwise loved his job. The people were great, and the work was engaging. Unlike other social media platforms, his employer was focused on trying to use technology to help users, not agitate them. But by the autumn of 2021, Arun was starting to get antsy. Perhaps sensing this, his boss called him in one day to deliver some exciting news. Finally—*finally*—Arun would be getting that big promotion. "You'll be receiving a raise as well," his boss said proudly. "No longer will you be making $75,000. In recognition of all that you've done for us, and noting, too, the enhanced responsibility you'll have in your new role, we're going to bump you up to $77,000!" He extended his hand. "Congratulations!"

Arun expressed gratitude, but as he left his boss's office, he was seething. He couldn't believe it. After five years and endless hours of great work, he got only $2,000 more? That wasn't a raise—it was an insult! Arun was done with this company and its exploitative ways. He was going to find an employer who truly valued him and was willing to pay him what he deserved.

As it turned out, other employment opportunities weren't hard to find. In fact, they were there for the taking. After meeting with his boss, Arun stormed home, hopped onto Glassdoor, and looked up what his peers at other firms were making. He also clicked on LinkedIn and within just a few minutes received a ping from a headhunter. A large investment bank was seeking to hire new talent for its social media department. Would he be interested in coming in for an interview?

Arun was an idealistic type—he wanted to do good in the world and didn't know if he'd find it fulfilling to work for a big bank. When he called me for advice, I told him that he should at least talk to the hiring manager to learn more about the opportunity. Arun agreed and went in for an initial interview. That went well and led in short order to several follow-up interviews. Just a couple of weeks later, the bank offered Arun a job with a starting salary of—get ready for this—$140,000 with a potential 20 percent performance bonus. That's right: Arun landed a new job that could more than *double* his current compensation.

If you're putting up with subpar treatment from a boss or an organization, I have one question for you: Why? During the pandemic, the labor market tilted decisively away from employers and toward workers. That became evident as millions of people in developed economies headed for the exits in what became known as the Great Resignation.[1] In

---

1 Abhinav Chugh, "What Is 'The Great Resignation'? An Expert Explains," World Economic Forum, November 29, 2021, https://www.weforum.org /agenda/2021/11/what-is-the-great-resignation-and-what-can-we-learn -from-it/.

September 2021, some 4.4 million American workers gave
their companies the pink slip—a new high.[2] That's 3 percent
of all workers quitting—in a single month.

Looking behind these numbers, we find that the pandemic recession had a seismic impact on the US labor force,
prompting workers at diverse income levels to rethink their
jobs and careers. Some weren't thrilled to return to difficult
jobs with low pay and no benefits. Many front line workers
felt burned out, while others focused on work-life balance.
This combination of factors upended the relationship
between workers and employers. With their wallets fatter
due to a combination of government pandemic assistance
and reductions in spending, and with more opportunities
at their disposal (that month, ten jobs were open for every
seven people who were seeking work), workers began moving toward their dreams.[3]

Of course, quitting might not be the right move for everyone.[4] If you generally like your job, boss, or company,
see strong prospects for advancement, or are not eager
to undergo the stresses of transitioning to a new organi-

---

2 Jennifer Liu, "A Record 4.4 Million People Quit in September as Great
Resignation Shows No Signs of Stopping," CNBC, November 12, 2021,
https://www.cnbc.com/2021/11/12/a-record-4point4-million-people-quit
-jobs-in-september-great-resignation.html.

3 Liu, "A Record 4.4 Million People Quit in September."

4 Amii Barnard-Bahn, "5 Reasons Not to Quit Your Job (Yet)," *Harvard
Business Review*, October 14, 2021, https://hbr.org/2021/10/5-reasons-not
-to-quit-your-job-yet.

zation and boss, you might do better to stick around in your current job but renegotiate your work arrangement in ways that matter to you. I playfully call this "bullying your boss."

Quit or Stay: A Quick Thought Experiment

Robbie Abed, author of the book *Fire Me I Beg You: Quit Your Miserable Job (Without Risking It All)*, has some advice for people trying to figure out if they should quit or if they might consider sticking around.[5] He recommends pondering the following scenario. Let's say your boss walks in right now and tells you that you're fired, not because you're performing poorly, but because of economic or business conditions beyond your control. How would you feel? If you would be elated, then you probably should leave right now if you possibly can. Your heart just isn't in it. If your feelings are more nuanced or ambiguous, then some further analysis might be in order. A second thought experiment: Take a hard look at the senior leaders in your organization and consider whether you would want their lifestyles. If you're revolted by how much they're working and how much

5 Robbie Abed, interview with the author, November 24, 2021.

> of their personal lives they've sacrificed for their jobs,
> then why are you continuing to devote your life to this
> organization or this line of work?

To some of us, the idea of forcefully advocating for what we want with our bosses and organizations seems anathema. Maybe we're not used to asserting ourselves, or we don't know how to go about it. Maybe we feel intimidated by our boss and fear that broaching certain requests would jeopardize our good standing. Maybe we know that our company has certain workplace policies in place, and we think we're powerless to change them. Women and people of color are especially prone to these feelings. As research shows, women are less inclined than men to aggressively advocate for themselves in the workplace.[6]

No matter what's hanging you up, I want to shake you out of complacency and inaction. You *do* have power—probably more than you think. Today, bosses practically expect you to stroll in and ask for a decent raise as well as the option of working from home two days a week. Some companies are so worried about employee turnover that they're proactively

---

6 Christina Pazzanese, "Women Less Inclined to Self-Promote than Men, Even for a Job," *Harvard Gazette*, February 7, 2020, https://news.harvard .edu/gazette/story/2020/02/men-better-than-women-at-self-promotion-on -job-leading-to-inequities/.

holding "stay interviews," soliciting employee desires and trying to satisfy them so that people won't leave.[7]

I can't guarantee that bullying your boss—whether at their invitation or not—will produce a great outcome. But I do know that one of my mother's favorite adages holds true: If you don't ask, you don't get. Regardless of how great the job market is, your boss might have more discretion to craft a job to your liking than you think, and they might also value you more than you think. Being savvy operators, they're probably not going to come right out and tell you that. To get more of the job-related goodies that you seek, you'll have to *ask* for them.

The BULLY Framework

The question, of course, is how? What's the best way to approach your boss to obtain what you desire? My simple advice is: *Don't wing it.* By putting in just a bit of time and doing your homework, you can lend more rigor to your negotiations, increasing the odds that you'll obtain what you desire. Get smart about your options and pursue them in a thoughtful, disciplined way—that's the path to success.

Based on my years of talking to professionals and their

---

7 Jennifer Liu, "Why the 'Stay Interview' Is the Next Big Trend of the Great Resignation," CNBC, updated November 30, 2021, https://www.cnbc.com/2021/11/30/why-stay-interviews-are-the-next-big-trend-of-the-great-resignation.html.

bosses, I've developed a five-step process for bullying any boss to get more of what you want. I call it my BULLY framework.

Bullying Your Boss

- **B**utton up your Big Ask
- **U**nderstand the full picture
- **L**ose the ego (sort of)
- **L**eave time to practice the conversation
- Don't **Y**uck it Up

Step #1: Button Up Your Big Ask

Before approaching your boss, clarify to yourself what you want. There are two important points to consider here. First, make sure you're considering the full array of possible requests you might make. When we think about negotiating with our bosses, our minds usually focus on the basics, like higher salary, access to health benefits, or more vacation. As important as these are, other components of the employment contract matter, too, such as signing bonuses, reimbursement for childcare, flexible scheduling, gym memberships, tuition reimbursement, sabbaticals, career development opportunities, and education loan repayment.

These perks are just some of the more common ones. In

today's economy, with so much in flux, employees can request perks that aren't so common but that might make an important difference in their lives. What about bringing your dog to work? Or having your employer offset some of the costs of setting up a home office? Or taking an extended leave to care for your ailing parent? Or having time at work to contribute to a charitable project on the company's behalf? Or exercising more autonomy on the job? Don't limit yourself to the usual parameters of employment. Get creative. And think about your pain points—the parts of your job that make life unpleasant. In an ideal world, or even in a not-so-ideal one, how could your employer help you to resolve each of these?

Take a step back and think about your deeper motivations. What *really* gets you jazzed about a job at this point in your life? Is it the size of your paycheck? Control over your schedule? The prestige of a certain job title? The existence of a pathway to career growth? The chance to do work that benefits humanity? The ability to work for a great boss or with amiable colleagues? Excellent healthcare coverage and other benefits?

If you care about multiple aspects of a job, as most of us do, try to prioritize them and weigh them against one another. If a company offered you a job with a great salary and the potential to move up in the organization, but this company had a business that was causing harm, would you still be interested? How does your current job rate against your top few priorities? If it delivers well against some but not others, might you push for concessions in those other areas that matter to you?

With these considerations in mind, take an initial stab at formulating the specific requests you'll make of your boss. You might decide that you want, as a best-case scenario, a 10 percent salary increase, or a promotion within six months, or five weeks of vacation each year instead of two. Think as well about what you might still be happy to accept, even if it isn't best-case—maybe an 8 percent raise this year and a 3 percent raise the year after, a promotion within a year as opposed to six months, and four weeks of vacation. And consider what your deal-breakers are—the requests that, if denied, would prompt you to walk away from your current job. If your boss offers only a 2 percent raise, would you say "See ya"?

You need not finalize your requests at this point—further analysis might prompt you to revise them. But before you go on, you should have a general sense of what leaves you underwhelmed about your current job situation and the steps your boss might take to fix it.

Pro Tip: Asking for a Pay Bump

Instead of asking for a specific number, propose a salary *range*, pegging the bottom of the range to the absolute minimum you'd accept. Proposing a range gives your boss a bit of wiggle room. Chances are, negotiations will land you near the middle of the range, but make a reasoned case for why you deserve to be in the upper part of the range. To maintain your credibility, base your range on what your research has shown to be reasonable. Salaries vary considerably depending on locale, so salary ranges you might find on the internet might not apply to you. Then again, with so many jobs going remote or hybrid, those differences are narrowing. Go beyond a simple search and consult with peers in your field and geographic region to find out what they earn.

Step #2: Understand the Full Picture

Once you're clear about your Big Ask, lay the groundwork for a successful pitch by doing some research. First, confirm that your requests are reasonable—or, on the flip side, ambitious enough. Gather various proof points and insights that will support you when you're making the pitch to your boss. That means taking some time to learn about the broader employment market, in your industry and beyond.

Mobilize your network to conduct this research, reaching out to others both offline and on social media. (Breaking news alert: People will tell you more in a simple phone conversation than they will when writing an email.) What do workers in your role generally make, assuming comparable experience, skills, and amount of responsibility? What kinds of special perks do they enjoy? Are you undercompensated or otherwise shabbily treated? Pay attention to the specific language that headhunters use when recruiting for positions like yours. Do they emphasize certain skills, experiences, or attributes that you possess and that make you especially valued in the marketplace? If you're dissatisfied with your firm, are conditions really that much better at the competition? What hidden challenges or opportunities exist there that only a company insider would know?

In addition, take an honest and comprehensive look at your own job and how you've performed. Have you really met or exceeded expectations in all areas? Have you contributed in additional ways that might not be reflected in your job description but were nonetheless important? Perhaps you created a new affinity group inside your organization for people who share your identity. Perhaps you came up with an exciting idea that doesn't help your business per se but another team has managed to monetize. Perhaps you've become the go-to expert on a given topic. Perhaps you've proven instrumental in helping the organization recruit a more diverse workforce. To grasp your true value, it's important to catalogue such elements.

I once brought in a million dollars in revenue for an employer, even though I wasn't working in sales at the time. I happened to know someone who knew someone, and acting on my own initiative, I used those connections to help my organization. My boss didn't know about these efforts of mine. Because I bothered to think through all that I had contributed, I was able to bring this accomplishment to her attention at bonus time.

Ask colleagues or trusted advisors how they perceive your

worth and what they think your assets and liabilities are as an employee. I did this myself not long ago. I was wondering if I was being undercompensated for my podcast, so I approached an expert in the field and asked him to review audience-related data from my competitors and tell me what he thought they were worth. Comparing his feedback with data from my own podcast, I concluded that I was being undercompensated, but not by much. The analysis didn't lead to any action on my part, but it was still helpful to have an accurate sense of where I was in the market.

Be sure as well to gather research about your boss and organization. How do they view you and your contributions? Are you making requests that are unprecedented or that directly contravene important company policies? Is now the best time to squeeze your boss for more goodies, given what is happening on your team or to the organization? In 2009, during the Great Recession, an employee expressed frustration to a friend of mine for not receiving a bonus after having requested one from her boss. Whether or not that employee performed well enough to merit a bonus, the timing of her request was absolutely nuts. When financial markets are crashing, the company stock is sinking, and your boss is struggling to handle the stress without her head exploding, you might want to wait on asking for a bonus.

When preparing for your Big Ask, consider whether you've really explored your options to the fullest. You might have researched your firm's direct competitors and how they treat their employees, but how might other employers in your industry or beyond value someone with your skills and expertise? Perhaps exciting but unconventional opportunities exist for you that you've overlooked.

A guy I know, Kenny, works for a distributor of alcoholic beverages. As he told me, his company and its competitors initially got clobbered during the pandemic as restaurants closed. Forced to reduce their employee headcount, they were unprepared to handle the rush of business as people began buying more liquor from retail stores. Kenny tried to hire back the employees they'd laid off, but he was still short of people.

He had a brilliant idea: He contacted a whole bunch of bartenders he knew who were out of work and asked them to work for him. Some of them hesitated at first, convinced that they knew nothing about sales. But as Kenny pointed out, bartenders tend to have great people skills, and because they spend hours each day talking to consumers, they have a keen understanding of who they are and what they want. If you think about it, Kenny told them, veteran bartenders might be better at selling than those who think of themselves as professional salespeople.

Kenny was on to something. At all times, and especially when labor markets are in flux, skills and experiences we've amassed in one area might prove surprisingly valuable in other areas. If you're a journalist, your writing skills might serve you well doing corporate communications for a pharma company. If you're a teacher who has spent a decade working with kids in the classroom, maybe a company making toys or apparel for kids would find you interesting.

Stop thinking narrowly about yourself in terms of your job title. Instead, consider more broadly what you actually *do* each day. What superpowers do you possess that contribute to your success? Maybe it's knowledge about a certain kind of product, market, or demographic. Maybe it's a soft skill, like the ability to negotiate, empathize with others, or lead a team. Whatever it is, identify your superpower and then start talking to people in your network, staying alert to other contexts in which that same competency seems to hold value. Even if less traditional opportunities ultimately don't appeal to you, knowing that they're out there can embolden you to step up and bully your boss with confidence.

Step #3: Lose the Ego (Sort Of)

With your research in hand, let's now consider how to craft a killer pitch. I only have one piece of advice, and it's one you've probably heard before: Don't be a jerk and overplay your hand. In delivering your pitch, come across as bold and confident, but don't appear arrogant, antagonize your boss, or put them on the defensive. Instead of focusing solely on you, keep your boss and *their* needs firmly in mind even as you convey your own desires. Lose the ego—sort of.

When you sit down to start the conversation, don't launch right into making your request and laying out your supporting arguments. Instead, prepare the way by referencing all that your boss and the organization have done for you and thanking them for it. So many managers I speak with describe feeling betrayed when employees approach them to negotiate better deals. They feel that newly empowered employees are shaking them down. I like to remind these bosses to consider how much loyalty, kindness, and respect they and their organization showed to this employee all along. But whether or not managers are correct in feeling betrayed, you serve your interests best by not triggering these feelings to begin with.

Swallow your pride and kiss up to your boss just a little. Even if you think your boss and the organization have mistreated you, be the bigger person. Certainly there's *something* they've done right. Start the conversation by focusing on that and expressing your gratitude for what you've been given.

When you get around to presenting the essence of your pitch, make it crisp and logical without overdoing it. Lay out a few key proof points as to why what you're requesting is reasonable and appropriate, providing quantitative data if possible. Let your boss see that you've done your homework and are informed, without appearing cocky or like a know-it-all. Balance out your pitch by empathizing with your boss, anticipating their concerns, acknowledging their legitimacy, and gently providing points and evidence from your research that suggest why your Big Ask still deserves consideration.

If you feel your boss hasn't quite met your needs in the past, guard against taking a negative or accusatory tone. You might feel tempted to say, "You've been underpaying me for years. Now it's my turn to squeeze everything I can out of you." Don't do this. Instead, explain that while you have been willing to work for less in the past because you love the company so much and care about its success, you now owe it to yourself and your family to make sure you get fair market compensation for your labor. Or describe how hard you generally find it to step up and ask for things, and convey that you're requesting a raise as part of your recent efforts to learn how to claim your true worth. Humanizing the conversation in these or other ways provides your boss an opening to empathize with you and your situation, lowering the odds that they'll respond defensively.

Relatedly, don't spend too much time claiming credit for all the amazing contributions you've made as a prelude to playing the victim and establishing how poorly you've been treated. It's important to reference your accomplishments, but temper such self-aggrandizement with a recognition of your boss's or organization's own challenges. If you work for a small company that your boss owns, perhaps they've struggled themselves financially, or if they haven't, perhaps they need to keep their costs low so as not to burn up too much precious capital. If you work at a larger firm, perhaps your boss has internal politics to deal with, including circumstances to which you're not privy. Keep these kinds of considerations in mind, and if it's appropriate, acknowledge them openly.

Step #4: Leave Time to Practice the Conversation

Once you've refined your pitch, you might want to charge right into your boss's office and deliver it. Not so fast. Since this conversation is a pretty big deal for you, it's important to practice it first. Deliver your pitch in front of a mirror or have someone take a video of you delivering it. Better yet, do what I do and role-play the conversation with a friend or relative, having them play your boss. If you're relatively young and your boss is older, ask a gray-haired person of your acquaintance to role-play with you (bonus points if it's someone who has experience serving as a boss). Take other steps to make the practice session as realistic as possible, such as dressing as you would on the job or including props like a cup of coffee in your hand. Arm your practice partner in advance with counterarguments to what you're proposing, and ask them to be as tough on you as possible within the bounds of reality.

Practicing a conversation might sound goofy, but it works. Not only might it help you feel more comfortable and speak more fluidly during the actual conversation, but it might also help you to understand your boss's point of view more deeply, which in turn will allow you to respond more persuasively on the spot.

Not long ago, I met up with the boss of a young woman whom I had counseled and who had negotiated with her boss and ultimately left her organization. As it turned out, the boss's perspective was nothing like what this woman had imagined.

The boss understood that this woman was unhappy with her job for very legitimate reasons, but she also felt that this employee didn't recognize that by leaving, she was also stepping away from an important commitment that she had made to her team. Although the boss accepted the woman's decision, she would have appreciated more empathy on the woman's part and an acknowledgment of how she was inconveniencing others.

Had the young woman role-played the conversation with an older person who had experience managing others, she might have uncovered this perspective. Because she hadn't, she had little sense of her boss's feelings. Her departure left a sour taste in her boss's mouth. This is never a desirable outcome if you can help it, especially in a fluid labor market such as today's. As your career progresses, you never know when you'll cross paths again with an old boss.

This young woman is hardly alone. When consulting with people who are negotiating with their bosses, I am continually struck by how little they really understand what the person on the other side of the table is thinking. Generational differences might play a role, and so, too, might a more generalized decline in empathy and rise of isolation in our society.[8] Make an effort to immerse yourself in your boss's way of thinking, even if it means rehashing high school drama class for an hour or two. Heck, it might even be fun!

---

8 "Decline in Human Empathy Creates Global Risks in the 'Age of Anger,'" Zurich, April 8, 2019, https://www.zurich.com/en/knowledge/topics /global-risks/decline-human-empathy-creates-global-risks-age-of-anger.

Step #5: Don't Yuck It Up

Even with solid preparation, you can never be sure how your conversation with your boss will go. Will you bully them, or will they wind up bullying you? In the latter case, please make sure you don't yuck it up (sorry, I'm trying to cut down on my cursing) by blowing your top and burning bridges.

It might feel good to lash out at your boss, but no matter how poorly they behave during your conversation, doing so is seldom in your long-term interest. Avoid giving your boss an ultimatum ("I'm leaving if you don't give me XYZ") when your softer entreaties fail to bear fruit. If your boss patronizes or insults you, smile at them and end the conversation in a respectful way. "Thank you," you might say, "this has been very informative." And then go home, pour yourself a stiff drink or three, drop as many f-bombs as you want to your friends, and start looking for a better job elsewhere.

If you've behaved poorly with your bosses in the past, don't sweat it. We all make mistakes. Many years ago, Reggie approached his boss to ask if she'd reconsider the bonus he'd been paid, which was half as large as what he believed he'd earned. In keeping with the advice in this chapter, Reggie did his homework, drawing on his network inside the organization to pin down the exact metric on which his bonus was based and who'd made the decision (his boss had). He also learned that all the conditions had been met—and then some—for him to receive a full bonus. His business unit had hit its objectives, and his individual performance had been fantastic.

When Reggie asked this manager why he hadn't received his full bonus, she responded that it was an unfortunate decision but that she hadn't made it—one of the higher-ups had. Reggie might have responded graciously to this bald-faced lie, but instead he got up into his boss's face and said, "Look, either you're a liar or you think I'm stupid. Which is it?"

It wasn't his finest moment, but thankfully, for various reasons that I won't detail here, it didn't wind up burning a bridge. Still, Reggie had risked damaging the relationship unnecessarily, and he had also failed to live up to his own standards. If there was ever a chance that his boss would walk away from their conversation, feel bad about what she did, and give him his full bonus, he'd scuttled that.

Many people behave immaturely not just during difficult negotiations with their bosses, but also afterward, upon leaving their organization. In exit interviews, they blame their lack of success on the company or the boss, lashing out at policies or decisions they disliked. Please don't let this be you. It doesn't cost very much to behave graciously. Maintain your dignity and do your best to stay calm and focused. If you can't tamp down your frustration or hurt feelings, then decline the request for an exit interview. Or as a friend of mine advises, "Lie like hell. If there is a boss you didn't like, be positive the whole way out. Never leave on bad terms or burn bridges because you never know what's going to happen next."

Even when it feels like your boss is bullying you back, resist the urge to behave vindictively. Express gratitude to the extent you can. Minimize the disruption that your departure will cause to your team.

Don't yuck it up.

The Unsung Virtues of Staying

Although Reggie's attempt to bully his boss yielded an unhappy outcome in the short term, it worked out great over the long term, providing the impetus he needed to make a major move in his career: After years of working for other people, Reggie finally decided to take a risk and go out on his own, doing the same work he'd come to love but as a free agent. Before long, he was making *more* money than he had been. And he hasn't looked back. If you ask him, he'll tell you that bullying his boss—or trying to—was one of the best things he ever did.

Many other people express similar sentiments, not because they wound up leaving their subpar jobs, but because they wound up negotiating a better deal and feeling better about showing up for work each day. Remember Arun, the guy who left after his boss ungraciously rewarded him with a paltry $2,000 raise? Well, another guy I know has a complementary tale to tell.

David, an attorney in his early thirties, made $150,000 a

year working at a midsized law firm in a large metropolitan city. His wife worked as a teacher, and between the two of them, they enjoyed a solid standard of living. One day, David received a call from a much larger firm offering him a job. The firm was staffing up, and having come across David's résumé, it wanted to bring him on board. The offer was attractive: The firm would pay David $200,000 and give him the option of working a few days a week from home. He'd handle the same workload as he currently was. A bonanza, right?

David felt grateful for the offer and was tempted to accept it. But since he liked his current firm, he opted to bully his boss instead of leaving straightaway. After giving careful thought to what he'd say, he went into his boss's office and told them about the offer. Instead of putting them on the defensive, he related that he really liked the firm and felt grateful to be working there, but since he and his wife were trying to start a family it would be really hard for him to turn down a $50,000 pay bump. His boss listened attentively and told him that they would see what they could do.

Knowing a bit about the firm's finances, David doubted his boss would be able to match the larger firm's offer. But as it turned out, they did. His boss delivered the news a few days later, telling David that they were able to match the offer; the firm's partners agreed that his work stood out above others at his level. With a $50,000 raise in hand, David opted to stay.

A Great Money Reset might well include a change in employment, but it need not. Get in the habit of advocating for yourself at work, making Big Asks and also a few smaller ones along the way. Do it when the job market favors workers, but also keep it in mind as a strategy when it doesn't. At all times, stay abreast of the job market and the potential opportunities that might exist for you, and understand what would *really* make your job work better for you than it currently does. Maintain a healthy sense of your own self-worth as an employee but refrain from going overboard and behaving arrogantly or angrily in making your requests. In other words, bully your boss, but do it respectfully and thoughtfully. You'll get more out of your job, and your boss will get what they want, too—a loyal, engaged, happy employee.

Rock the Reset

- You may have power as an employee, so don't be afraid to bully your boss. If you don't ask, you don't get.

- Deploy the BULLY framework: **B**utton up your Big Ask; **U**nderstand the full picture; **L**ose the ego (sort of); **L**eave time to practice the conversation; Don't **Y**uck it Up.

- Make a habit of advocating respectfully for yourself at work, making both large and small requests.

4

Invest in *You*

When you're undergoing a Great Money Reset, or in general grappling with volatile economic times, your investments can make all the difference. Put your money in vehicles that keep your nest egg stable and protect you from the downside while also allowing you to participate in the upside.

What were you doing at 11:20 A.M. on October 11, 2021? Sarah Robison, a forty-year-old nurse anesthetist living in Pittsburgh, Pennsylvania, was at the top of Mount Katahdin in Maine, sore feet and all. As hiking enthusiasts know, this mountain isn't just another pretty peak (and boy, is it pretty). Rather, it marks the northern end of the Appalachian Trail, which begins way down south in Georgia. Over the past six months, Sarah had traveled all of the trail's 2,193.1 miles by foot, traversing mountains and stopping off at towns and other sights along the way. Now that she had reached the end of the line, she celebrated her incredible and unlikely journey, reveled in all that she'd accomplished, and pondered its meaning.

Sarah has a simple rule, one that many of us would do well to follow: Live uncomfortably. She's not talking about doing without air-conditioning, forgoing deodorant, or taking cold showers—at least, not necessarily. She's talking about overcoming our fears. When a particular situation or course of action leaves her feeling scared or intimidated, she doesn't avoid it but instead leans into it. Whereas most of us flee from our fears, staying close to what is familiar, she chooses to open herself to a range of new experiences.

In setting off on her hiking adventure, Sarah put this rule into practice—big-time. With a pandemic raging, she did something many people would consider crazy: quit her stable, well-paying job to pursue a dream. She would travel alone, for the most part, and blog about her experiences to the world. To fund her expedition, she would use a portion of a $50,000 nest egg she had been saving for the down payment on a house.

Had the trauma of working in healthcare during the pandemic gotten to her? As Sarah told me, it hadn't, and she also wasn't trying to heal some terrible wound she had suffered, à la Cheryl Strayed of *Wild* fame. All in all, she was in a pretty good place in life. But like other people in this book, she found

herself reflecting on what truly mattered to her. Because she
had been a disciplined saver from her earliest work years,
she was financially comfortable. And without a life partner
or kids, her only obligation was to herself. But what was the
point of continuing to work like a dog to maximize her financial wealth? "It sounds clichéd," she told me, "but I was like,
'I want less stress and more happiness.'"

Sarah had a feeling that tackling the Appalachian Trail—
and also making herself vulnerable through her blog—would
increase her happiness and in general bring positive change
to her life. She had been heading in this direction for some
time. A couple of years earlier, having had little experience
with hiking, she spent a few days on the trail and instantly
became smitten with the sport. During that trip, she walked
into a visitors' center and happened to see a photograph
of a man who had summitted Mount Katahdin. She found
the intensity of emotion on his face both arresting and in-
spiring. "It changed me to see this photograph, and I honestly said to my friend, 'I want to do whatever it takes to
feel this way.'"

Now, standing there atop Mount Katahdin on day 270 of
her expedition, she felt "a spiritual experience" all her own.
As she recounts in her blog, she arrived at a wooden signpost
that marked the trail's end and experienced a sense of "my
evolution of self. My confidence. My courage. My strength.
My fearlessness. My acceptance. My patience. My wander-
lust. My willingness. My dedication. My grit. My pain. My

faith. My trust. I did the thing. The *f$&@!#g* thing. Which was, to let go."[1]

It wasn't simply that Sarah had fought through pain, doubt, and inclement weather to finish the entire hike on foot, something that most hikers on the trail don't accomplish. It's that she had overcome her fears of quitting her job and the stable life it had provided to pursue a dream. She had taken a risk and let go.

But it wasn't an irresponsible risk. Prior to embarking on her quest, she had performed the rigorous financial analysis that I've recommended, even consulting with a financial advisor. As the advisor confirmed, quitting her job might impact her retirement savings, but it wouldn't compromise her future. You see, in addition to saving and paying off her student loan debt, Sarah had maxed out on her retirement contributions since the age of eighteen, taking advantage of partial matches offered by her employer. By the time COVID hit in early 2020, she had already amassed $400,000 in well-balanced, target-date funds. And all of that savings was *on top* of a pension that her employer provided. That's not too shabby for a single person with a couple of decades or more still to work.

Like reining in spending, making smart investment decisions proves critically important for people undertaking significant money resets. Disciplined investing can enable

---

1 Sarah Robison, "And on the 207th Day, She Rose," *On the Appalachian Trail & a Life Unconventional* (blog), October 20, 2021, https://www.andtheniwalked.com/blog/day-207-she-rose.

you to make major life or career changes without jeopardizing your entire future, and it can also help you navigate times of uncertainty, such as those touched off by the pandemic. And yet, many people find investing during these periods of flux quite confusing. They wonder whether the ordinary rules still apply or if they must adjust their investing strategies to reflect changing conditions.

As I see it, the rules do still apply, with some interesting tweaks. If the pandemic taught me anything, it's to value the present more than I once did, and the future a bit less. Yes, I've loosened up a little. The old Jill would have urged you to maximize your long-term savings so that you can enjoy as much financial opportunity as possible in the future. The new Jill recognizes that life can be short, and while we do want to sock away what we can and invest it prudently, we should also factor the value and quality of our time *today* into our decisions.

In other words, we should invest in *us*, in ways that go beyond money and that embrace both the present and the future. Maybe we do want to sacrifice some retirement savings to feel the thrill of summiting Mount Katahdin, or to start a new business venture, or to retire early from a successful but soul-crushing career and explore another side of ourselves. Maybe we do want to risk a small portion of it on a seemingly crazy investment opportunity that, if it bears fruit, might change our or our loved ones' lives.

If you're contemplating a money reset, the trick is to allow yourself to grasp tantalizing but risky opportunities that might arise while at the same time pursuing proven invest-ment strategies that will allow you to continue to amass long-term wealth. To explore how to best achieve this balance, we must delve into some of the specifics. Here are the *seven investing questions people ask me most frequently* when pon-dering a Great Money Reset, as well as my latest thinking on how to answer them.

Question #1: Conventional Wisdom Holds That Passive or Index Investing Is Best. Is That Still True in Volatile Times?

Darn straight it is. As I argued in my previous book, indexing (where you buy a fund that mirrors a specific asset index, such as the S&P 500 stock index or a bond or commodity index) really works, no matter what's happening in the wider world. You might shake your head at this, objecting that you're bet-ter off putting your money in the latest hot stock du jour. In 2021, that might have been Tesla, which during the decade after its founding saw its stock price rise more than 4,000 per-cent.[2] How can the S&P 500 or some other boring old index possibly compete with that?

I'll tell you how. None of us knows in advance how a given

---

2 Lora Kolodny, "Tesla Stock Is Up More than 4000% Since Its Debut 10 Years Ago," CNBC, updated June 29, 2020, https://www.cnbc.com/2020/06/29/tesla-stock-up-4125percent-since-ipo-ten-years-ago.html.

company will perform. To lower their risk, most active investors (people who buy and sell stocks on an ongoing basis hoping to outdo various indices) avoid investing in one company and instead buy a basket of stocks. When you do that, it becomes very difficult to outperform market indices over long time periods. Robin Wigglesworth, a journalist with the *Financial Times* who just happens to have the coolest name ever, wrote an authoritative book on the history of index funds. As he related to me, "The math around indexing is irrefutable." Sure, an actively managed fund might beat an index in a given year, but will it outperform consistently over a long period?[3] Most of the time it won't.

Periods of flux often leave us craving more certainty and control, and we might feel inclined to satisfy that craving by actively managing our investments. If you're playing around with some fun money, no problem (more on that in a second). But when we're talking about your retirement holdings or your kid's college fund, go with what the actual data say and stay passive. Some areas of our life require a great deal of sophistication and thought on our part. This isn't one of them. If you're undertaking a big change in your life, such as a new job or a move to a faraway city, isn't it nice to know that you don't need to freak out about your

---

3 I recount this argument in "Indexing Withstands the Test of Time," *Jill on Money* (blog), October 27, 2021. See Robin Wigglesworth, *Trillions: How a Band of Wall Street Renegades Invented the Index Fund and Changed Finance Forever* (New York: Portfolio/Penguin, 2021).

investments—that you can just continue to sit tight and let the markets do their work?

The key to sound investing isn't to be a genius, staying one step ahead of markets. It's to *not blow it* by avoiding unforced errors. Don't follow those who are looking for the next rocket-ship stock. Slow, steady, and passive wins the day.

Question #2: What's the Deal with Crypto and Other Hard-to-Understand, High-Risk, Volatile Investments? Are Those Verboten?

Ah, crypto. The old Jill would have taken one look at the stuff (which of course you can't really see), held her nose, and said, "Don't get involved in *that*." In fact, I did say that for the first five years that I covered crypto. But the new Jill says, "Hey, don't bet the farm. But if you'd like to put 5 percent of your holdings into the cool idea du jour, whether it's an NFT (non-fungible token), a SPAC (special purpose acquisition company), or cryptocurrency, what's the harm in that?" Times of change in the broader society bring new opportunities. When we're undergoing change ourselves, we're more open to novelty. Why fight that? We should allow ourselves the chance to grasp some of these opportunities, within reason, and not berate ourselves for being rash or irresponsible.

I want to credit one of my listeners, Taylor from Virginia

Beach, for helping me to broaden my thinking in this area. When Taylor called me in April 2021, he told me that he was at an "existential crossroads." He and his wife were both forty, their child would be off to college soon, and they were ready to launch themselves into a new phase of life. Taylor was a little sick of his grind at an IT firm. He was willing to work at another company and perhaps in another role, but he didn't want to feel the pressure of bringing home a certain amount.

As Taylor detailed the couple's finances, I became increasingly excited for him. Disciplined savers, he and his wife had amassed $850,000 in 401(k) and IRA accounts. They owned their $400,000 house outright. They had saved $70,000 in a 529 account for their child's college. They had amassed about $100,000 in cash. And get this: Several years earlier, Taylor had taken $10,000 from an old 401(k) and, on a lark, invested it in bitcoin. "I have long advocated that this is a ridiculous thing to do," he told me. Maybe, but that $10,000 now was worth—get ready for it—a cool $1 million. In addition, the couple had used earnings from bitcoin to pay off their house.

Taylor and his wife were in an excellent position to pursue a Great Money Reset, not because they'd foolishly plunged all of their investment assets into a novel, high-risk investment, but because they'd wagered a relatively small portion of those assets that, in a worst-case scenario, they could afford to lose. Taylor's biggest problem now was figuring out how to cash out of bitcoin while minimizing his tax exposure and accessing the extra cash he'd need over the next decade if he downshifted his career. That was easy: He needed to roll some of it into an IRA while taking smaller portions out as cash over time, staying within the bounds of what the tax law allowed him to withdraw with a zero percent capital gains tax rate.[4]

We shouldn't all necessarily rush to buy crypto. But those who do like to get in on the latest innovative investing opportunities and who kick themselves when they fail to take the leap should feel free to invest. The way I see it, if you've been a diligent and smart investor and put the bulk of your money in a passive index fund, then you're entitled to take a flyer with some small portion of your portfolio, so long as you're comfortable with possibly losing that money. Who knows, you might get lucky and see a big gain, like Taylor did, one that can facilitate your Great Money Reset. Contrary to what the old-school fuddy-duddies in the investing world might say (yeesh, do I resemble those folks?), it's not at all wrong to live a little and take a risk or two. Just don't let it get out of hand.

---

4 In 2022, a married couple filing jointly pays no capital gains tax if their income is $80,800 or lower. Between $80,801 and an income of $501,600, they pay 15 percent tax. If their income is above $501,600, the taxman taketh 20 percent ("Topic No. 409: Capital Gains and Losses," IRS, accessed May 5, 2022, https://www.irs.gov/taxtopics/tc409).

Question #3: How Should I Handle My Investments in Company Stock? Should I Continue to Buy It at a Discount?

Mike and Erin, a married couple from New York, called in with an innocent question about whether they were well positioned to retire in a couple of years. Boy, did they get an earful.

Overall, their situation was *awesome*. Mike had spent twenty-eight years working in tech, while Erin didn't work. Both were fifty-three years old, and the couple had no kids. Combined, they had a net worth of $3.2 million, with $2.8 million in retirement and non-retirement investments. The two lived on $3,500 a month, and upon his retirement Mike would receive a pension of $3,500 a month. In short, the couple had everything they needed to maintain their current lifestyle indefinitely, and quite a bit more.

It was when I asked Mike and Erin to run through their investments that my hackles rose. Every year, Mike's company had paid him a portion of his total compensation in company stock. Rather than sell off enough of that stock to maintain a balanced portfolio, Mike had continued to hang on to it—perhaps out of inertia, or because he liked the company. So far, he had accumulated $800,000 in company stock—a whopping 25 percent of his and his wife's net worth.

That's nuts! A sound investment strategy calls upon us to maintain no more than 10 percent of our portfolio in any single holding. Otherwise, we're assuming too much risk.

In his defense, Mike noted that his company had performed well in the past year. But while I had them on the line, I was curious how the company had done over the past five years, so I looked it up. I discovered that the company's stock was up 70 percent over that time—good, but not nearly as good as the S&P 500, which had risen over 110 percent. Excessive attachment to the company had cost the couple 40 percent in additional earnings they might have realized had they simply dumped the money in an index fund.

There's no reason to go heavy on company stock. Almost always, the upside won't be as profitable as the downside is scary. That's true even if you're buying your company stock at a discount. Bear in mind that often you must hold company stock for some period of time before selling, so you're locked in during that period even if the stock tanks. Buying stock at a discount protects you somewhat from losses relative to the rest of the market, but think about how crappy you'll feel if you buy that discounted stock and it drops precipitously. Remember all those Enron employees who hung on to the stock as it soared, only to be left in the dust after the company's bankruptcy?

Whether you receive a discount or not, protect yourself on the downside and keep no more than 10 percent of your holdings in company stock. Most CEOs believe in their company, and yet so many of them don't hesitate to sell blocks of their own company's stock on a periodic basis. Why is that? Because they understand the need to take some risk off the table. If you've been robotically amassing stock from your company, now is the time to act like a CEO and finally lower your risk. Make *that* a part of your Great Money Reset. Sell off a portion of your stock over the next few years, or all of it at once if you like (depending on your tolerance for capital gains taxes). Drop that money into a diversified portfolio of index funds, and watch it grow.

You might object that you absolutely *love* your company, agree with its values, and want to support it in your investing. Values-based investing is laudable. We should all do our part to save the world, and we might feel especially inclined to do so now, when we're taking steps to make our lives in general more meaningful to us. But we must be careful not to compromise our own futures. If you hold excessive amounts of company stock, you're effectively piling risk on top of risk. If your company experiences a setback, not only might its stock lose some obscene percentage of its value, but you might also lose your job. Now you're doubly screwed. That's never a good situation, especially in times of change, when markets and economies are more volatile.

If you really want to invest according to your values, consider putting money in a fund that invests in socially responsible companies. The challenge here is that it's not always easy to measure the social impact of these companies reliably, so as an investor, you might not be getting what you think you're getting.[5] Still, more socially responsible funds are popping

---

5 For a largely skeptical analysis of ESG funds, see James Mackintosh, "Why the Sustainable Investment Craze Is Flawed," *The Wall Street Journal*, up-

up all the time, and low-cost funds of this ilk can serve as a good starting point.[6]

Question #4: If Interest Rates Seem Poised to Rise, Should I Still Be Investing in Bonds?

Many investors feel reluctant to purchase bonds in an environment of rising interest rates, because higher rates lead bond prices to fall.[7] Why should you buy an asset whose value will decline?

There's a very good reason. Owning bonds isn't really about making a bet on the direction of overall interest rates. It's more about lowering volatility in your overall portfolio and providing relatively *predictable* returns over time. Own-

---

dated January 23, 2022, https://www.wsj.com/articles/why-the-sustainable-investment-craze-is-flawed-11642865789.

6 I discuss socially responsible investing in my article "Green Your Investments," Synchrony Bank, accessed April 12, 2022, https://www.synchronybank.com/blog/millie/green-your-investments/. For a guide to low-cost socially responsible funds, see Katherine Lynch, "Where to Find Low-Cost ESG Funds," Morningstar, June 6, 2020, https://www.morningstar.com/articles/987495/where-to-find-low-cost-esg-funds.

7 Why do rising interest rates cause bond prices to drop? Easy. If you bought a US government bond paying a given interest rate, and interest rates rise, newly issued government bonds will pay higher rates to lenders. Ergo, your older, lower-rate bond will drop in value. See "Back to School for Your Money: Bonds," *Jill on Money* (blog), accessed May 5, 2022, https://www.jillonmoney.com/blog/back-to-school-for-your-money-bonds-kmhew.

ing bonds can allow you to buffer big losses in equity markets, which, as we know, can occur when we least expect them. To optimize your portfolio's performance over the long term, you should own both stocks and bonds at all times, even when interest rates are heading higher.

A glance at the historical performance of portfolios that contain varying compositions of stocks and bonds might surprise you. Look at the decades between 1926 and 2020. The investment firm Vanguard tracked how well a portfolio of 100 percent bonds did against one composed of 20 percent stocks and 80 percent bonds.[8] The company also considered portfolios that were more heavily weighted toward stocks, including those composed entirely of stocks. A portfolio with a 60/40 stock-to-bond ratio yielded an annualized return of 9.1 percent over that roughly century-long period. Guess what annualized return a portfolio that was all stocks yielded? Was it 15 percent, or maybe 20 percent?

An all-stock portfolio yielded an average annual return of just 10.3 percent. You might have done slightly better if you ditched the bonds entirely, but not necessarily. Other factors come into play, including human emotion. Most investors who own a large portion of stocks grow anxious when the market drops precipitously. All-stock portfolios saw some crazy-bad years over the past century, the worst being in 1931, when their

---

8 "Vanguard Portfolio Allocation Models," Vanguard, accessed April 12, 2022, https://investor.vanguard.com/investor-resources-education /education/model-portfolio-allocation.

value dropped 43.1 percent. That same year, a portfolio that was 60 percent stocks and 40 percent bonds dropped only 26.6 percent in value—also the worst year over the course of the century for that kind of portfolio. The risk in owning all stocks and forgoing bonds is that you'll freak out and bail during the down times. That, of course, would be precisely the wrong thing to do, locking in losses. Your long-term performance will suffer in turn.[9]

We can think of the roughly 1 percent difference in long-term performance between an all-stock portfolio and a more balanced one as a small fee we pay to protect ourselves from doing something stupid. We need to stop ourselves from taking action during the tough times, and bonds can help with that. It's tough to predict whether interest rates will rise and bond prices fall over the next few years. What I do know is that people who stick with diversified portfolios don't get itchy when the you-know-what hits the fan. Diversification is a great strategy in "normal" times, and an even better one in periods of flux. Again, in your drive to exert more control over your life, don't make the mistake of overthinking your investment strategy. Just as you want to stick with passive investing, you also want to stay well diversified. Some areas in life really do require a periodic makeover. Not this one.

---

9 "Vanguard Portfolio Allocation Models," Vanguard, accessed April 12, 2022, https://investor.vanguard.com/investor-resources-education /education/model-portfolio-allocation.

Question #5: To Improve My Ability to Make a Great Money Reset, Should I Sell Off Investments to Pay Down Debt, in Particular My Mortgage?

The answer is: It depends. Let's say you have $50,000 in federal student loan debt outstanding at a 6 percent interest rate. During the pandemic, the government put such loans into forbearance, effectively reducing the interest rate to zero and freeing borrowers from the need to make repayment. Let's further say you kept your job during the pandemic, so you had extra money on hand—the funds you saved on your monthly loan payment and perhaps a stimulus check you received from the government. You could have used all of this money to pay down your debt anyway, but instead you put it in the stock market. Over the course of a year, that $7,000 turned into $12,000. But that was just luck, not smarts—and probably not the wisest decision. In most cases, you should keep any money that you believe you will need within a year in a safe, boring, interest-bearing account.

That said, once forbearance is over and you must make monthly payments again on a 6 percent loan, should you use that $12,000 to pay it down? Absolutely. Should you sell other, non-retirement investments to pay down this debt as well as any high-interest credit card debt you might have? Absolutely. Should you sell retirement investments (assuming you're above the age of fifty-nine and a half), paying the required taxes, to pay down your low-interest mortgage? No friggin' way.

In the last scenario, you would be liquidating a portion of your precious retirement savings, which might have been earning 5 percent, 7 percent, or more. In so doing, you would be on the hook for the ordinary income tax liability applicable to what you withdrew. Is it worth pulling money from an account and paying the tax due just to pay off a mortgage that might have cost you only 3 percent a year in interest? Further, as I've emphasized elsewhere in this book, individuals who are making significant transitions in their lives should strive to maximize their liquidity if they can. By paying off the mortgage, you've lost liquidity. Far better to keep this money in your retirement savings, where it will continue to work for you and where you can potentially access it if you need to.

When they reach inflection points in their lives, many people want to pay off mortgages for the psychological lift they'd feel at no longer having to make a big monthly payment. If you're so wealthy that you have plenty of cash rolling around and you wouldn't miss the earnings you'd forgo, then perhaps you can cash out and pay off that debt for the sake of preserving your sanity. Even then, be clear about what you're doing. Using retirement savings to pay off a mortgage could potentially cost you tens of thousands in lost earnings. Is that the best way to ease your mind? Or would investing in a good therapist or a weekly massage to ease your stress be cheaper and more effective?

I like to think of "good debt" as an obligation you have that works for you, both financially and in other ways. I'd consider a low-interest mortgage to be relatively good debt, since you can deduct the interest from your taxes and the debt allows you to live in your home and put other funds you might have to work for you. A student loan is also good debt, to my mind, since even if it's expensive it allows you to gain an education and potentially earn more in the future (not to mention pursue a more enjoyable and fulfilling career). A credit card balance is bad debt, since it isn't working for you—it's just costing you dearly. Most of the time, you will have already consumed the goods you purchased with this debt (you've already taken the fancy trip or eaten the expensive meal out). You're not leveraging these goods to open up new opportunities for yourself. And the money you're paying to service that debt is lost to you for investment purposes.

Pay off bad debt if you can, but if you have good debt that costs less in interest than you would make by investing over the long term and that allows you to retain access to cash, then keep that debt in place. Paying off that mortgage might seem attractive now, and if you're making only 1 percent on your retirement savings, maybe it's not a terrible move. But even then, what if something bad were to happen five or ten years from now and you needed cash? Because you've sold off your retirement investment, you might not have the funds you need. Interest rates also might have risen considerably by then, making it more expensive to borrow. You'd be screwed, all because you let your emotions get the better of you.

Question #6: Let's Say I'd Like to Retire Early as Part of My Great Money Reset. Must I Really Lower the Riskiness of My Investments in Retirement?

Conventional wisdom says you should, but I say not necessarily. Let's remember what retirement savings are for: to cover your expenses once you're no longer working so that you can live the life you want. Before you can understand how much risk to continue to take with your investments, you must understand your needs and how much you might reasonably withdraw from savings each year during retirement to meet them.

A quick-and-dirty way to think about this is to assume that you can safely withdraw $30,000 to $35,000 each year for each million you have in retirement savings (in other words, 3 to 3.5 percent of your holdings). With that level of withdrawal, you probably won't exhaust your savings during your lifetime. (This is not an exact science—if you want the real numbers, you'll have to use a more sophisticated retirement planning calculator.) If you have $5 million in your portfolio and only run about $50,000 in expenses each year, then you're not depending on every penny of the approximately $150,000 you might withdraw from your portfolio. You might decide to take more risk with at least a portion of that portfolio, reasoning that the earnings will allow you to leave more to your kids and grandchildren.

A similar analysis holds if Social Security and a pension cover your needs and your retirement savings are extra. You don't necessarily need to lower the risk, since even if you were to suffer short-term losses, you wouldn't jeopardize your retirement. On the other hand, you might well decide to move toward a low-risk strategy, since again, it doesn't really matter to you if you grow your money.

My point here is to get you to look beyond easy, overly simple rules and take a more nuanced and personalized approach to risk. Even if you're younger, you might not want so much investment risk simply because it freaks you out. If you're doing great at your job and earning enough to sock more away in retirement savings to make up for what you might have earned using a riskier investment strategy, then forgo the risk. If you're younger and don't mind risk, then it's fine to opt for a riskier strategy.

Pay attention to *you* and what keeps you happy. Over time, your investment strategy will probably drift in accordance with your natural inclinations regarding risk. We don't need to mess with that. All we need to do is give you some basic guardrails to consider so that you don't blow yourself up and have a sucky retirement. Save enough and take on enough risk in investing so that you'll have enough to draw on when you're older. Plan on drawing down no more than 3 to 3.5 percent of your holdings each year. Stick within those guardrails, and you'll probably be fine.

Question #7: In Times of Cultural Change, with Many Nontraditional Sources of Advice Available and Traditional Authorities Under Siege, Whom Should I Turn to for Financial Advice?

A ton of financial advice comes at us these days. We've long had guidance from several sources: opinionators in the media (who, *moi*?), newsletters, the informal advice we might have received from personal acquaintances, the professional advice a Certified Financial Planner might have provided. Today we also receive an endless stream of advice from Reddit communities, YouTube channels, Twitter, TikTok, and the like. Some of this advice is rife with conflicts of interest, and understanding whom or what to believe can prove a daunting task. It's especially hard to know how much credence we should give to what we hear from random people on social media.

Here's what I say: When it comes to investing your fun money, by all means, feel free to check out what the folks on your subreddit of choice think. You might even want to listen to them. Beware, of course, that you're entering the mosh pit of investing—there are some super-smart people on there, some who have no idea what they're doing, and others who have an agenda and are trying to hype one investment idea or another. Sift through what you encounter with a keen and skeptical eye. Try to poke holes in what you hear and not become too emotionally invested. Remember that the wisdom of the crowd might win out over the short term, such as when it comes to picking the next meme stock, but it might not win over the long term.

When it comes to your real-money accounts, like your work-based retirement plan or your supplemental taxable retirement account, you'll probably want to turn to more credible, reliable sources. If your finances are relatively straightforward, try advisors on platforms like Vanguard Personal Advisor Services or Betterment. At each, you will be prompted to take a brief risk assessment quiz, and an algorithm will do the work of managing your investments. For a small fee, you'll also get financial advice that is solid and uncomplicated and that most of the time will do the job.

If you have a more complex financial life, you may want to seek professional assistance. Ditto if you've experienced a major financial event, whether good (you've received a windfall) or bad (a spouse or parent has died), or if you're contemplating a major financial move (such as the sale of a piece of property or a change in your retirement plans) as part of your Great Money Reset. It's not a bad idea to continue to consult a financial advisor if you simply feel stressed out about money and would like a qualified professional to lead you by the hand. As I've said elsewhere, a smart financial advisor can make an enormous difference, potentially saving you tens of thousands of dollars or even more and giving you piece of mind.

If you're undergoing a Great Money Reset and you've worked with a financial planner in the past, it might behoove you to ask another professional to review your finances. At this turning point in your life, it can help to make sure you're getting the best advice, especially if you're making a change with complex tax or other implications. Even if you love your planner and swear by their wisdom, you never know what another set of eyes might uncover.

For years I relied on an accounting firm to prepare my taxes. Risk-averse by nature, I liked that this firm took a conservative approach. Once I moved to New York, I asked a different Certified Public Accountant (CPA) to review some of my past returns to make sure that I wasn't missing anything. He pointed out that my situation had changed: Whereas I was once an employee, I now worked as an independent contractor. As a result, he was surprised to see that my previous firm had not advised me to take a home office deduction, to which I was entitled. As he informed me, the tax code envisioned this deduction for precisely someone in my situation. Taking it wasn't an aggressive move at all. This one change saved me tens of thousands of dollars each year on my taxes, and I never would have uncovered it had I not solicited a second opinion.

Other friends and acquaintances of mine have had similar experiences. In one case, a financial review uncovered a $100,000 mistake on a friend's tax filing in his favor. My friend's longtime and beloved family CPA had simply missed it.

In many cases, a financial review won't uncover any big mistakes or opportunities. Rather, it will just confirm that you're already getting excellent advice. That's helpful, too. If you're embarking on a Great Money Reset, feeling certain that you're on track will give you a bit more peace of mind. You'd solicit a second or third opinion if you were contemplating a big medical move, like getting a major surgery or embarking on treatment for a serious illness. Why not do it with your money?

They're Rules, Not Guarantees

Now that we've run through these questions, I hope you're in a better place not simply to invest as you pursue a Great Money Reset, but to invest in *you*. As we've seen, the basic rules of investing when attempting a major life or career shift are very much the same as they always were. You need not radically reinvent your strategy—in fact, you shouldn't. That said, there are a few nuances to understand if you are to make the most of the years ahead while also grasping opportunities today. You should also be aware of an important caveat. To convey it, I must tell one final story.

Joseph, a longtime colleague of mine at CBS, was sixty years old and nearing retirement. Over the years, I repeatedly advised that he should sell off portions of his Viacom-CBS stock to remove excessive risk from his portfolio. Did he listen to me? Not at all. He kept pooh-poohing my advice and making excuses. Of course, every time the stock fell on hard times, he freaked out and resolved to sell when the stock came back up. Yet he never did.

Fast-forward to the spring of 2020. ViacomCBS (now

Paramount Global), which had been trading in the $30–$40 range, fell to under $12 per share. Predictably, I got a hysterical call from Joseph, who wanted to know if he should sell his stock. I asked him if he needed the money right now, and he said he was hoping to retire soon but had a separate retirement account that was doing okay. We ran the numbers, and his situation was pretty clear: Joseph needed to keep working for about five more years to have enough for retirement. In the meantime, he had to hang on to the stock and wait for it to go up.

During the months that followed, ViacomCBS recovered a bit, rising above $20. I called Joseph and asked if he'd sold off any of the stock, and he replied that he hadn't. At the end of 2020, with the stock trading in the high $30s, we spoke again. He told me he knew he had to sell, but he was just so tired and distracted, he didn't want to deal with it just then.

During the early months of 2021, ViacomCBS became ensnared in a strange trading scheme engineered by a family investment fund, and these machinations sent ViacomCBS's price soaring. By March, the stock was in the $70 range.[10] Colleagues at CBS started calling me to ask what

10 Juliet Chung and Maureen Farrell, "Ex-Tiger Asia Founder Triggers $30 Billion in Large Stocks Sales," *The Wall Street Journal*, March 28, 2021, https://www.wsj.com/articles/ex-tiger-asia-founder-triggers-30-billion-in-large-stocks-sales-11616973350; Neal Freyman, "Wall Street Mystery Swirls over Massive Block Trades," Morning Brew, March 28,

was going on, and I told them emphatically that they should sell. I texted Joseph as well and conveyed this message. A week went by without a response from him. Then another. Finally, he texted back with a screenshot and the message, "Phew. Just sold." Guess how much he sold it for? A whopping $90 a share.

As Joseph later told me, he hadn't carefully timed the sale. He had decided to sell in the $70s when he had received my text, but he hadn't gotten around to it. On the particular day when he'd finally managed to sit his butt down and do it, the price had risen. And just days later, the stock price collapsed back down into the $30s. Joseph had gotten really, really lucky. Since he held 5,000 shares of ViacomCBS, his total sale was worth $450,000. If he had sold at $13 a share about a year earlier, he would have netted only $65,000.

The sum of $450,000 was a game-changer for Joseph. Now he could embark on his Great Money Reset and retire early instead of waiting until age sixty-five. As it turned out, Joseph opted not to retire, but he did decide to leave his demanding job for a less stressful, lower-paying position at a nonprofit.

Let's ponder this for a moment. We started the chapter with Sarah, who was well positioned to quit her stressful job and hike the Appalachian Trail because she had done everything by the book. Joseph, by contrast, did quite a bit *wrong* in managing his investments. For years he held way

2021, https://www.morningbrew.com/daily/stories/2021/03/28/wall-street-mystery-swirls-massive-block-trades.

too much company stock. His neglect could have come back to bite him, but it didn't. In the end he walked away with almost half a million dollars. Life just isn't fair.

And that's my point. You can play by the rules of investing or ignore them, and in the end you can never be sure what will happen. Your fortune could take a sudden turn for the better . . . or for the worse. Good sense dictates that we play by the rules most of the time rather than tempt fate, since we stand the best odds of realizing our goals. But even if we do play by the rules, we must prepare ourselves mentally for anything to happen.

My wish for you is that despite whatever dumb moves you've made, you experience an unexpected windfall like Joseph did. Failing that, I hope you at least make sound investing decisions that *most likely* will give you the freedom you need to embark on your next great adventure. Invest in *you*—you can't afford not to. But do it, as always, with your eyes wide open.

Rock the Reset

- The ordinary rules of investing do apply in times of uncertainty and upheaval, with an important tweak: Let's loosen up a bit. Enjoy the present a bit more while also securing your future.

- Consider seven key topics: passive investing, crypto, company stock, bonds, paying down debt, investing in retirement, and whom to solicit for investing advice.

- Play by the investing rules, but prepare yourself mentally for anything to happen. Because it can—and it has.

5

The IRS Is Your Friend

No, seriously. In this chapter, we'll explore how to use the tax code to your advantage to help you fund your big move.

Of the many financial topics out there, there is one that is so hot, so sexy, so incredibly satisfying, so completely irresistible, that it always makes for great radio. I'm talking about Roth IRAs. Okay, I'm being sarcastic, but Roth IRAs really are much more interesting than you'd think, and they're also potentially important to you as a financial planning tool.

Consider a call I received in late 2021 from Steve in Boston. Months earlier, Steve's wife, Christina, lost her job, foisting a Great Money Reset onto the couple unexpectedly. Come tax time, fifty-six-year-old Christina would claim only about $20,000–$25,000 in income from state unemployment benefits—a fraction of what she had made before. Fortunately, the couple's overall finances were strong. Fifty-seven-year-old Steve brought in about $200,000 from his job. The couple had $1.8 million in retirement savings ($1.2 million in Steve's account and $600,000 in Christina's) and $600,000 in a brokerage account, as well as $100,000 in a Roth IRA. Their $1.2 million house was paid off.

All told, Steve and Christina were in great shape to retire in six or seven years, as they'd planned. They had some juicy pensions that would yield $100,000 per year, and they expected to receive $50,000 in Social Security between them— more than enough to cover their monthly expenses without even touching their retirement savings.

Given this scenario, Steve wanted to know if he should convert a part of his traditional retirement savings account into a Roth account before the end of the year. Mindful of his retirement plans and their unusual situation due to his wife's layoff, he wondered if there was an opportunity to save some money going forward on taxes.

He was absolutely right—there was—and here's why. Many people undergoing Big Money Resets anticipate temporary dips in income due to changes they're making (or, as in Steve and Christina's case, that are imposed upon them). Maybe they're leaving well-paying jobs they hate for others that pay less but are more fulfilling and less stressful. Maybe they're taking some time off to hike the Appalachian Trail, enjoy a cross-country adventure, or go back to school. Whatever the case, a drop in income might create an opportunity to lock in their future tax liability now, since they'll likely be in a lower tax bracket today than they will in the future.

This advice might strike you as odd. What about that old rule of thumb about retirement planning—that you should defer paying taxes until later, since your tax bracket likely will be lower in retirement? That thinking used to make sense, but it's quite possibly out of date. As I write this in 2021, most tax rates are at historically low levels, which means that it is likely that brackets have nowhere to go but up. In this context, front-loading your taxes might prove a desirable step.

The primary vehicle for handling future tax liability in the present is a Roth IRA, the 1997 iteration of that popular retirement savings vehicle, the Individual Retirement Account (IRA). In the original IRA (now called a traditional IRA), you deposit money tax-free and pay taxes years or decades later when you take distributions from your account, at whatever your tax rate is at the time. A Roth IRA is deliciously different: You pay the tax due now on the funds you deposit in the account, and the money then grows tax free. Later in life, when you're ready to withdraw funds, you owe *no* additional taxes. Also, you're not forced to take money out of your account every year during retirement (and pay taxes at those times), as you are with a traditional IRA starting at age seventy-two. These required minimum distributions (RMDs) can be surprisingly large (if you have $4 million in an IRA, for instance, you might be required to withdraw $146,000 at age seventy-two, just the beginning of the RMDs that would be due). Say hello to some hefty tax bills.

Good news: If you have money hanging around in a traditional IRA, you can convert it to a Roth IRA. You can tell the IRS, "Hey, man, I want to take a chunk or all of this traditional IRA retirement money, pay the tax that's due right now, and then not have to pay anything later." In Steve and Christina's case, performing a conversion made sense: Christina's job loss lowered their combined income, so they would probably be taxed at a lower rate now than in future years. They could also minimize future RMDs from their traditional IRAs later in life. As many people find, these distributions are problematic not just because they require paying tax, but because they push your income up later in life, potentially causing your income-tested Medicare premiums to rise. By converting funds to a Roth, Steve and Christina could avoid these problems and feel more certain about their future tax liability.

The question for Steve and Christina then became how much of their retirement savings they should convert and pay taxes on in 2021. The answer: as much as they could without pushing themselves into a higher tax bracket (since any money they're converting counts as income). But there was a big caveat: Steve and Christina also must have enough cash on hand to pay the extra taxes they would accrue because of the conversion and still have enough liquidity left over for an emergency fund and other needs. Liquidity is paramount; you don't want to blow through all of your cash just to gain these goodies from the IRS.

By my calculation, Steve and Christina would be taxed at

a top federal income tax rate of 24 percent given their lower
combined income in 2021. They could convert about $100,000
to a Roth IRA without bumping up to the next tax bracket
of 32 percent. And they could cash out some of their non-
retirement investments to pay the extra taxes, taking advantage of a fairly low capital gains rate of 18.8 percent. In the end,
making these moves might well save the couple thousands of
dollars in taxes they would have had to pay in retirement—
all because they knew to take advantage of an opportunity
created by a Great Money Reset.

Most of us presume that thinking about taxes is boring—
and compared with gawking at cat pictures on Facebook or
rewatching *Mare of Easttown*, I suppose they are. What we
might not fully appreciate is how life or career changes might
create opportunities for us to save money or at least achieve
more certainty about our tax burdens. No matter what our
politics are or how we feel about taxes, we owe it to ourselves
to take advantage of the provisions afforded to us by our tax
laws. The money you save or the certainty you gain might
make a Great Money Reset more practicable. You might be
able to retire earlier, take a job that pays less, or enjoy a higher
quality of life in the years ahead—all because you understood
what the tax law allows and took advantage of it. The IRS
very well can be your friend during a major money reset, but
only if you know what to do.

Take Some Pain out of Your Capital Gain

Benefitting from your temporarily low tax bracket by converting to a Roth IRA is a powerful financial tactic, but there are others to know about—like strategically taking a capital gain on an investment you have. Let's say you haven't listened to Aunt Jill and are sitting on a pile of company stock. Or maybe you've got a tidy sum that has been growing steadily in a taxable brokerage account. You might be looking at a frightful tax bill some years down the road when you cash out and take the gain. Since long-term capital gains tax rates are pegged to how much you make (you pay either zero, 15 percent, 18.8 percent, 20 percent, or 23.8 percent), it might make sense to take advantage of your lower income and pay the tax now.[1] Again, you'll

---

1 There were three basic capital gains tax rates in 2022. "The tax rate on most net capital gain is no higher than 15% for most individuals. Some or all net capital gain may be taxed at 0% if your taxable income is less than or equal to $40,400 for single or $80,800 for married filing jointly or qualifying widow(er). A capital gain rate of 15% applies if your taxable income is more than $40,400 but less than or equal to $445,850 for single; more than $80,800 but less than or equal to $501,600 for married filing jointly or qualifying widow(er); more than $54,100 but less than or equal to $473,750 for head of household or more than $40,400 but less than or equal to $250,800 for married filing separately." "Topic No. 409: Capital Gains and Losses," IRS, accessed April 12, 2022, https://www.irs.gov/taxtopics/tc409. The feds also assess an additional 3.8 percent Medicare surtax on net investment income if your modified adjusted gross income (MAGI) is above $200,000 as an individual or $250,000 as a married couple filing jointly. "Topic No. 559: Net Invest-

likely save money, since capital gains rates are not especially high in historical terms and that means they very well might rise.[2] At the very least, you'll gain more certainty about your tax liability and potentially avoid unpleasant surprises later. If you hold an asset for less than a year, then the gain would be taxed at your ordinary tax bracket, so it may behoove you to either wait until a year has passed or you drop into a lower bracket. And don't forget to factor in any losses that you might be carrying forward from previous years.

Let's say you and your spouse have a $300,000 capital gain from a cryptocurrency investment. You previously had earned $150,000 between the two of you, but in 2021, with only one of you working thanks to a money reset, you earned a combined $75,000. That's enough to drop you from the 15 percent long-term capital gains rate to zero. If you're sitting on a big, fat capital gain that has been building in a Coinbase account for a while, now is an incredible time to take the gain—you stand to save tens of thousands of dollars if you do it this year as opposed to later, when your spouse is working again and your income has rebounded back to around $150,000.[3]

Bear in mind, if you're an art collector and you have a big

ment Income Tax," IRS, accessed April 12, 2022, https://www.irs.gov/taxtopics/tc559.

2 During the late 1970s, the top long-term capital gains tax rate reached 40 percent. In 2022, it was 23.8 percent.

3 "Frequently Asked Questions on Virtual Currency Transactions," IRS,

capital gain on that rare Renoir you bought some years ago, this analysis doesn't apply to you. The government taxes long-term gains from the sale of artwork at a higher rate than those mentioned above—we're talking a 28 percent rate, plus a 3.8 percent net investment tax.[4] For different reasons that I'll explain in a moment, you also probably won't benefit from a temporary reduction in your capital gains rate if you notch a profit on the sale of your home. But many of us with long-term capital gains to pay might well make out great by taking advantage of the decline in income that comes with making a Great Money Reset.

Living Like Kings in Queens

In addition to using a Great Money Reset as a springboard to ease the tax burden from our retirement savings and capital gains, we should also consider the potential tax ramifications of important changes we're thinking of making to where we live and how we work. For example, many of us set up home offices during the pandemic—another area where the IRS might turn out to be surprisingly simpatico.

Rachel and her husband, Larry, have about $600,000 in a

accessed May 5, 2022, https://www.irs.gov/individuals/international-taxpayers/frequently-asked-questions-on-virtual-currency-transactions.

4 "Topic No. 409 Capital Gains and Losses," IRS, accessed May 5, 2022, https://www.irs.gov/taxtopics/tc409.

traditional retirement account and $500,000 in Roth accounts. In a good year, they earn a combined income of $250,000–$300,000. In 2021, they earned only about $150,000. Could they take advantage of their lower income to move some more traditional retirement savings to Roth? Absolutely. But that was only the starting point for their Great Money Reset tax adventures.

During the pandemic, Rachel began to work from home more often (Larry, a graphic designer, had previously done so). Seeing as the two of them lived in a small apartment, life was getting a little crowded. By a happy coincidence, their neighbor in the adjacent apartment put his flat up for sale. Should they buy the apartment and use it to create offices for the two of them? Maybe, but maybe not. The place was a wreck. Their neighbor, who had lived there for the past few decades, had been a low-grade hoarder who lived out of boxes and failed to make minor repairs (when tiles broke in the bathroom, for instance, he fixed them with duct tape). Since the apartment lacked a working bathroom and kitchen, no bank would loan them the money. They would have to pay cash for the place and then renovate the heck out of it.

That's exactly what Rachel and Larry did. Whereas their own apartment was worth $450,000, they were able to pick up the neighbor's place for only $300,000 (remember when the sky was falling and experts were predicting the end of cities?). It cost them about another $100,000 to renovate it. Rather than knock down a wall and combine it with their apartment, Rachel and Larry kept it separate and used it strictly for office space. She took a bedroom in the neighbor's apartment as her space, while Larry took the living room. They intended to use the neighbor's space as offices for perhaps the next fifteen years until Rachel retired, selling it off thereafter.

Was this purchase a good move? Probably. The couple needed the extra space, and they had the spare cash to make it theirs. But the tax benefits were also enormous. If we're using part of our home as an office, we must be careful about what percentage of our home we're actually claiming as office space. Claim too much, and the IRS might crack down on you. Since the new apartment Rachel and Larry bought was clearly separate from the one they had been using as their home, they could treat it as an office property, which entitled them to depreciate it over time, a tax planning coup. They could also either deduct the renovation costs or add them on to the apartment's value, increasing the cost basis when calculating capital gains on a future sale of the apartment. In the latter case, they would have lower capital gains, meaning lower taxes once they sold the place. Going forward, they also could deduct all of the costs they would accrue in keeping the second apartment, including electricity, cable, modem, maintenance, property taxes, and so on. All of this would amount to a considerable tax savings, which made the purchase an even better deal for the couple.

Home offices are an obvious place to look for tax benefits, but at the present time they apply only if you're self-employed. If you're employed, you can't deduct costs related to setting up a home office that you, not your employer, accrue. It used to be that you could deduct them, but the 2017 tax law passed under the Trump administration did away with that provision for employees from 2018 to 2025.

It's funny: Many people fear paying *more* in taxes if they were to become self-employed, since the IRS taxes you both as a business and as an individual. In fact, the deductions to which you become entitled when you're self-employed often make it quite attractive from a tax standpoint. These include not only expenses related to home offices but other costs essential to earning income, including professional services (legal, accounting), computer equipment, transportation, and travel.

Self-employed people can also adopt retirement plans that carry some nifty advantages. For example, the Simplified Employee Pension IRA (SEP-IRA), which is geared toward those who have up to twenty-five employees, allows you to sock away up to 25 percent of your self-employment earnings.[5] There is a ceiling here: Your allowed contribution maxes out at $61,000 for 2022, with a $305,000 limit on compensation.[6]

---

5 To calculate this, take your net profit and then subtract 50 percent of what you paid in self-employment taxes and what you set aside for your SEP account. For more on SEPs, see "Simplified Employee Pension Plan (SEP)," IRS, May 5, 2022, https://www.irs.gov/retirement-plans/plan -sponsor/simplified-employee-pension-plan-sep.

6 Jill Schlesinger, "Retirement Plans for Self-Employed," *Jill on Money* (blog), accessed April 12, 2022, https://www.jillonmoney.com/blog/2019 /9/9/retirement-plans-for-self-employed-59g6w; "Simplified Employee Pension Plan (SEP)," IRS, accessed April 13, 2022, https://www.irs.gov /retirement-plans/plan-sponsor/simplified-employee-pension-plan-sep.

And whatever percentage you wind up putting away for your own retirement, you must also give the same to each of your eligible employees.[7]

You might also opt for a solo 401(k) plan, perfect if you have lots of funds to put toward savings and don't have anyone working for you (a spouse is okay).[8] The solo plan allows you to defer up to $20,500 of compensation in 2022 (or $27,000 if you're age fifty or above). You can do this as a Roth contribution or pre-tax.[9] The IRS lets you contribute another quarter of what you earned from working for yourself, up to a grand total of $61,000 for 2022 (make that $67,500 if you're age fifty or above).[10]

If you're bringing in the big bucks and want to save large amounts for retirement, then setting up an individualized pension plan might be an attractive option. These so-called defined benefit plans are a bit complex, and they cost a lot— you'll need to set aside funds for a number of years to get

7 "Simplified Employee Pension Plan (SEP)," IRS, May 5, 2022, https:// www.irs.gov/retirement-plans/plan-sponsor/simplified-employee-pension -plan-sep.

8 "One-Participant 401(k) Plans," IRS, May 5, 2022, https://www.irs.gov /retirement-plans/one-participant-401k-plans.

9 "Retirement Plans FAQs on Designated Roth Accounts," IRS, May 5, 2022, https://www.irs.gov/retirement-plans/retirement-plans-faqs-on -designated-roth-accounts.

10 "Publication 560 (2021): Retirement Plans for Small Business," IRS, May 5, 2022, https://www.irs.gov/publications/p560.

them going and keep them chugging along. But this outlay of resources might be worth it. With defined benefit plans, you can save up to $245,000 each year pre-tax, and you can make a 401(k) contribution to boot![11]

I would never start a business solely for the tax benefits. After all, you must earn income—in other words, have a viable business—before deductions and juicy retirement plans start to matter. But if you're toying with the idea of leaving a full-time job and going off on your own, the tax picture is definitely worth considering.

Whether you work from home or not, *where* you choose to live also carries tax implications. If your employer gives you the option of working remotely, you might choose to move from a state like New York, where taxes are relatively high, to a state like Texas, which has no state income tax (and fewer government-provided services as well). Pay attention to the details here: Working at a company based in New York City, for instance, might mean that, as an employee, you still must pay steep New York City taxes even if you live elsewhere (there's a price to pay for living or working in what New Yorkers call "the center of the world"). Also, if you're thinking of leaving a company and working as a

---

11 "Retirement Topics—Defined Benefit Plan Benefit Limits," IRS, accessed April 13, 2022, https://www.irs.gov/retirement-plans/plan-participant-employee/retirement-topics-defined-benefit-plan-benefit-limits.

freelancer, the locality where you live might levy a special tax on unincorporated businesses.

If you're thinking of selling your house to move to a lower-tax environment, you should also understand the ramifications that might occur from that sale. Happily, many of us wouldn't have to pay a hefty capital gains bill—or even *any*—when selling homes that have appreciated. If you're married and you satisfy certain conditions, you pay no tax on the first $500,000 in profits (or the first $250,000 if you're single) you realize from selling your primary residence. I find it amazing—and strange—that the IRS allows this exception for real estate gains. In what other class of assets do we allow people to make profits without paying tax on the gains? It seems unfair that we'd allow home buyers a free pass on taxes once they sell and notch a gain, whereas that same money invested in the stock market would yield a taxable gain. We're favoring homeowners at the expense of renters, in my opinion—and for no good reason.

That said, if you're selling your home, you should take advantage of this idiosyncrasy in our tax laws. When planning a Great Money Reset, it helps to know that you won't have to pay thousands or even tens of thousands of dollars in taxes on the sale of your house. By the same token, if you and your spouse are realizing a mammoth gain from the sale of your home (you bought it for $200,000 and are selling it for $2 million, for instance), you should factor in that only the first $500,000 of the gain will be tax free. The rest of it will be subject to long-term capital gains taxes, which could amount to quite a significant bill. This might not scuttle your Great Money Reset, but it's important to plan for it.

Nice People Finish First

Yet another way the IRS might become your friend—or at least friendlier—during our Great Money Reset has to do with charitable giving. Let me preface this by observing that the vast majority of taxpayers, about 85 percent of us, generally don't see great tax benefits when they give to charities. Only if you itemize your deductions, which the wealthiest 15 percent of Americans tend to do, can you take deductions for charitable donations you make. (There is one exception to note: The CARES Act of 2020 allowed people taking the standard deduction to take up to a $300 deduction for individuals and a $600 deduction for married couples for charitable donations in 2020 and 2021.)[12]

---

12 "Year-End Giving Reminder: Special Tax Deduction Helps Most People Give up to $600 to Charity, Even If They Don't Itemize," IRS, November 3, 2021, https://www.irs.gov/newsroom/year-end-giving-reminder-special-tax-deduction-helps-most-people-give-up-to-600-to-charity-even-if-they-dont-itemize.

If you do itemize your deductions, here are *four key tactics* that might help you improve your tax outlook as you contemplate or undertake a Great Money Reset. Observers sometimes disparage these tactics as gifts for the wealthy, but so long as the tax code allows for them, you should feel perfectly comfortable using them—they are legit.

Tax Tactic #1: Donate Highly Appreciated Stock

Sure, you could give cash to your favorite charity and lower your tax burden by deducting that donation from your income. But let's say you worked for Amazon during the 1990s and 2000s and as a perk received a bunch of stock that has since been sitting around in a brokerage account. Since Amazon's stock price has risen so precipitously (the split-adjusted IPO price in 1997 was $1.50 and the price at the time of this writing was about $3,000), that stock is now worth a small fortune. That's wonderful, but it's also a problem: You know that selling it will create a huge tax bill.

One solution is to gift some of that stock to your favorite charity instead of cash. The charity can immediately sell the stock and put the resulting monies to good use. Because they're a nonprofit, they don't have to worry about paying taxes. Meanwhile, you get to deduct the entire value of the stock *and* you need not pay any capital gains on it. If you're looking to make a major transition in your life and you want to lighten your tax burden, this is a great way to do it (assuming you have some appreciated stock lying around).

Tax Tactic #2: Bunch Your Donations

Let's say that as part of your Great Money Reset you've decided to sell your expensive home and rent for the foreseeable future. Perhaps you're normally the kind of person who has plenty of itemized deductions to take related to your home (state and local taxes, mortgage interest, and so on). After you sell your home, you might find it better to take the standard deduction while you're renting, since you no longer have all of these big itemized deductions to take. You might presume that during these years you can't make charitable donations and deduct them from your taxes. You'd be right.

Let's say, however, that you also have a piece of property that you're selling at a sizable gain—a rental property you own, for instance. You know you're going to get a big tax hit that year, and you'd like to find ways of minimizing it. One technique you might try is what the experts call "bunching your itemized deductions." The year that you're going back to itemizing your deductions, you can give away a larger chunk of money, what you might have given over a period of several years. You can tell the charities involved that you are giving them a gift that covers the next three, five, or however many years, and you can take this larger deduction in this one tax year when it will bring you the greatest benefit.

This tax trick assumes that you're inclined to give charitably. If not, then bunching your donations and the associated deductions won't seem so attractive. But if you are charitable and you would donate the money involved anyway, then bunching your donations strategically could save you thousands or more that you otherwise would have paid to the IRS. As the old saying goes, give to get.

Tax Tactic #3: Open a Donor-Advised Fund

Here's a slightly different way to give to get. Let's say that as part of your Great Money Reset you receive a windfall. Maybe you take a new job and make a new salary of $1 million, or maybe you inherit a tidy sum from a relative, or maybe you sell your home and notch a gain. You've got assets in hand, you know you won't need all or much of this windfall to live on, and you know you're going to have to pay taxes on it.

Let's further say that you're charitably inclined and would like to live your values by donating $100,000 over the next several years or longer. You could open a vehicle called a donor-advised fund and pop that $100,000 in there. Doing so would allow you to take a one-time deduction of $100,000 this year. Then you could use this fund to dribble out donations in the years to come. The following year, for instance, you could grant $20,000 to one charity. The year after that, you could grant $10,000 each to three different charities. And so on and so forth. Once you've set up the fund, how and when the money goes out is up to you. You do have to give all the money away eventually, but it doesn't have to happen immediately or even in your lifetime (one caveat is that you usually have to make grants every few years). If the fund still exists at the time of your death, you could leave instructions in your estate documents for someone to give the money away afterward.

For a person undergoing a Great Money Reset, donor-advised funds are a powerful way to ensure that you'll be able to continue to give years down the road, even if your income or assets decline. If a donor-advised fund sounds like a rich person's device, please know that it doesn't have to be. Financial services firms today make it easy for anyone to create these funds and then afterward to make donations from them.

I opened one of these accounts myself through Fidelity Charitable. As the end of the year approaches, I can look on my phone and determine what I gave the previous year to a slew of charities. I can also easily search for new charities and locate their tax ID numbers. With a couple of clicks, I can push money out to my selected charities—it couldn't be easier. You can also deposit highly appreciated securities into a donor-advised fund. The stock automatically converts to cash that you can donate, and as stated previously, you avoid paying the capital gains and can deduct the current market value of the securities from your taxes.

Tax Tactic #4: Take a Qualified Charitable Distribution (QCD)

A friend of mine, Joelle, is seventy-five years old and looking at taking a required minimum distribution of $15,000 from her retirement account. Joelle's pension, Social Security income, and income generated from her brokerage accounts more than cover her monthly expenses, so she doesn't need the money from the RMD and would rather not pay the associated taxes. What she can do is divert the $15,000 required distribution and send it straight to one or more charities in what is called a qualified charitable distribution (QCD). When she does that, she avoids paying any taxes on that $15,000 RMD.

If you're making a Great Money Reset, you're charitably inclined, and you're over the age of seventy and a half, a QCD is a great tax planning tool. You're going to want to donate a certain amount each year to charity anyway, and you might be worried about the tax burden represented by all of those RMDs. With QCDs in your back pocket, you can put your mind at ease by channeling money toward charity in a tax-advantaged way. The only hitch with QCDs is that the charity must cash the check in the same year for you to qualify for the exclusion.

Taken together, the tax tactics I've presented here are a terrific set of tools to have at your disposal. If you're younger and working and sitting on appreciated company stock, you can get a nice tax break by donating all or a portion of it. Bunching donations and opening donor-advised funds are excellent ways to help you reduce your tax liability if something great happens to you and you get a windfall. And it's wonderful for those of us nearing retirement age to know that we can use qualified charitable deductions to reduce the tax burden that comes with required minimum distributions from our tax-deferred retirement accounts. Relatively few people know about these tactics as they embark on major changes in their lives. Now that you do, don't hesitate to use them. You'll be glad you did.

Leaving "The Best Job in the World"

For some of us, the pandemic has been a wake-up call to get off the career treadmill and do more to help others. We want more enriching, fulfilling work—a career that makes a difference. But what if you're already helping to save the world? One of my callers, Ellen from Minnesota, fell into that category. For years she worked as a nurse ministering to victims of sexual assault, more recently as a nurse supervisor. It was an emotionally challenging role, but Ellen loved it. "It's the best job in the world," she told me. "Every day I go to work, I make a difference."

In the past, Ellen couldn't imagine retiring, but at age sixty-four she decided that she would finally make the move in about a year's time. She had found another way of giving back: She would spend more time caring for her elderly mother, who suffered from dementia. In addition to retiring,

Ellen saw the need to change her living situation. As of 2021, she shared a $1 million home with her sister and her mother. Ellen and her sister planned to sell the home (which was entirely paid off) and each buy co-op shares in a community for those fifty-five and older. Ellen's mother would continue to live with her, but now Ellen wouldn't have to spend so much time taking care of a big house—the co-op would handle that.

Ellen dialed me up because she was concerned about how she would be able to swing the move to the co-op. She and her sister would need two years to sell their house. When it sold, Ellen would have more than enough cash to afford the $300,000 to $350,000 that a co-op share would cost. But co-op shares weren't easy to procure—Ellen was on seven different waiting lists. If one became available before her house sold, she would need to snap it up, and she wasn't sure how she would get the cash without paying a boatload of taxes.

When I asked Ellen about her assets, she told me that she had a tidy sum—$1.4 million—in traditional, tax-deferred retirement accounts. In addition, she had $65,000 in cash, $60,000 in a health savings account (HSA), and $160,000 in a Roth IRA. Although she wouldn't qualify for a pension upon retiring, she would have an annuity she had purchased that she intended to draw upon starting at age seventy. Between the annuity and Social Security, she would cover her monthly expenses.

Running through these numbers, I saw Ellen's quandary: She had enough money for retirement, but the bulk of her funds hadn't been taxed yet. If she had to take $350,000 out of her traditional retirement accounts to cover the purchase price of her new co-op apartment, she would pay taxes on that amount—a scary proposition indeed. I didn't want her to use all of her previously taxed savings to buy the house, thus lessening what she would take out of her tax-deferred savings. She needed ample stores of cash on hand in case her mother suffered an unforeseen setback or some other emergency cropped up.

Ellen's situation dramatizes what could happen to us later in life if we don't attend to our future tax liability along the way. One day we might find ourselves in a situation where our options are constrained not because we don't have enough money, but because using our hard-earned money will saddle us with hefty taxes. We might still be able to pursue a Great Money Reset of our choice, but at a cost that would be greater than we'd like.

None of this, of course, is meant as a criticism of Ellen's choices. She amassed her retirement nest egg by saving diligently. For whatever reason, she hadn't been able to take some of the tax burden off the table. But for many of us, as we've seen, options do exist that allow us to minimize our tax burden. We can use a Great Money Reset as an opportunity to convert tax-deferred retirement funds into Roth savings or to take capital gains now, lowering our tax burden later. We can also manage our tax burden in the present, making our Great Money Reset more financially attractive for us by deducting home office expenses, strategically moving to a lower-tax location, and using a variety of vehicles to achieve tax savings via charitable donations.

Ellen was fortunate—she had options available to her that would allow her to generate the cash she needed without running up her tax bill. Notably, Ellen could take out a home equity line of credit (HELOC) to help her bridge any gaps in time between when she needed access to cash and when she'd have it from the sale of her home. As co-owner of her home, her sister would have to sign off on this, but Ellen was confident that she would (her sister already had plenty of money to spend on her own co-op apartment).

I advised Ellen to prepare for her move by stockpiling as much cash before her retirement as she could. She should funnel off a portion of her paycheck for retirement, but only enough to qualify for the maximum matching contribution from her employer. After that, she should save up as much cash as possible. During the four years before she turned seventy, she should also try to convert some of her tax-deferred savings to a Roth IRA, paying the required tax. Considering that she was in the 22 percent tax bracket, she shouldn't prioritize this. Taxes probably wouldn't rise that much over the next several years for someone in that bracket, and it would protect her and her mother if she maximized her cash on hand.

I admire Ellen for making such an important contribution to the world via her work and for stepping up to take care of her mom. But Ellen also deserves kudos for managing her own affairs responsibly. Not only was she a great saver, but she also was clued in to the tax rules enough to understand and worry about her likely obligations. All of us should ponder our tax situations as we plan major changes. We often treat the IRS as our enemy, but when you're contemplating a major life or career change, the IRS can indeed be your friend. I don't know about you, but when it comes to ensuring my financial comfort, I want all the friends I can get.

Rock the Reset

- The IRS can be your friend during a Great Money Reset.

- Optimize tax brackets; consider a Roth IRA conversion; strategically harvest capital gains; look for business-related tax benefits; and consider the tax ramifications related to charitable giving.

- Maximize charitable giving by donating highly appreciated stock, bunching your donations, opening a donor-advised fund, or executing a qualified charitable distribution.

6

Put Your House in Order

You might find yourself waking up in the morning and thinking, "Hmm . . . today is a good day to buy or sell a piece of real estate." But if you're contemplating a Great Money Reset, is it really?

Spending more wisely, bullying your boss, making smart investment decisions, taking advantage of the tax code: All of these actions might put you in the best possible position to change your life and move toward your dreams. But there's another big action you might want to take, despite the emotional pain it might bring: selling what is likely your biggest asset, your home.

In 2020, my listener Marilyn from Buffalo, New York, found herself in an extremely rough spot. Her beloved husband of over forty years, Patrick, had passed away two years earlier, sending her into the throes of mourning. With the pandemic raging, Marilyn now found herself beset by a terrible loneliness. She had a network of friends and family, but she couldn't see them, nor did she have any children to keep her company. "I spent Thanksgiving and Christmas Day alone," she recalled, "and it wasn't nice. We were in the height of the pandemic, and it was really bad in western New York."

But even as she struggled, Marilyn was girding herself to make some important changes. Shortly after Patrick died, she had retired from a successful career in banking and taken on part-time work as an internal auditor. Now, at age sixty-five, she decided that she would leave this role and realize her longtime dream of buying a place in Florida. "This is the winter of my life," she told herself, "and I want to spend it as healthy as I can and with as much fun and happiness as I can, too." Moving to a Florida retirement community would allow her to escape the harsh Buffalo weather and enjoy golf, swimming, and social opportunities.

As she was pondering this move, one question facing her was what to do with her present home in Buffalo. Selling it would be extraordinarily painful. She and Patrick, a professional decorator, had built it together, and he had decorated it beautifully from top to bottom. Letting it go would be one more step in coming to terms with her tragic loss.

And yet, as Marilyn ran the numbers, she realized that selling was the right thing to do. Her annual taxes on the property were substantial, amounting to more than her mortgage payment (after all, this is New York State, whose motto could be "We Heart Taxes"). Moreover, with housing prices rising in Buffalo just as they were throughout the country, it had become a seller's market. Given the potential sale price, she would likely be able to afford to buy not one but two new homes: a smaller townhouse in Buffalo and a condo in Florida. She'd be able to live as a classic snowbird: enjoying the beautiful western New York summers and flying south each year as the weather grew colder.

In 2021, after a great deal of financial analysis and soul-searching (including a few therapy sessions), she made her big move. Selling her home for $375,000, she paid off her $100,000 mortgage balance and bought two new properties. To her surprise, she was able to keep her part-time job, which paid for her health insurance; without Marilyn even asking, her boss offered to let her work remotely from Florida.

When I spoke with Marilyn months after her sale, she reported feeling that she was in a good place both financially and emotionally. The combined mortgage payments for her two properties ran her only one-third of what she had been paying each month on the home she'd shared with her husband. Between Patrick's life insurance, her own retirement savings, and Social Security, she had engineered a comfortable retirement that allowed her to maintain a foothold in the community where she had lived most of her adult life while also exploring a new locale. Although it was still early days, she had developed a small but nice group of friends in Florida and was looking forward to meeting more people at her new retirement community. Since an acquaintance of hers had bought her Buffalo home, she knew that these new owners were taking good care of it, making it much easier to let go emotionally. "It has all worked out beautifully," she told me.

In times of dramatic change, real estate can underpin a sound financial strategy, enabling you to make a Great Money Reset that might otherwise have proven elusive. We observed this during the pandemic, when a booming real estate market created opportunities for many homeowners to fund early retirements, geographical moves, career changes, and other major life moves by tapping their equity. But even when markets tighten, smart real estate moves might still enable you to make important progress in your life. The key is to stay in touch with your emotions. (Emotions again? Yup, sorry!)

Many of us harbor fears and attachments that might prompt us to hold on to real estate too long or wait too long to buy. I'm no shrink, but I have listened to a lot of callers talk through their anxieties about their beloved homes, only to follow up with me off-air to tell me they finally were ready to act. Though it's painful, if we work on our entrenched fears and transcend them, we might find that buying or selling a piece of real estate can bring us surprising happiness, fulfillment, and growth as part of a Great Money Reset. "I've learned that everything you really want to accomplish in life is on the other side of fear," Marilyn said. Pretty profound wisdom, if you ask me.

An Exciting New Life Down on the Farm

Marilyn had a particular dream in mind: retiring to Florida. What if you want to make a change but you don't yet know what you want out of life's next chapter? Can buying or selling real estate still make sense?

Tom and Pam, a married couple from suburban Pennsylvania, would answer with a resounding yes. As front line healthcare workers (Pam is a nurse, Tom a physical therapist), the two were feeling burned out in their careers, having witnessed the horrors of the pandemic firsthand. Adding to their stress, the couple felt exhausted from running on what seemed like a financial treadmill. They were swimming in debt, making payments on their mortgage, a home equity loan, their kids' student loans, and significant credit card balances. To crack their monthly nut, Pam would often feel compelled to take on overtime shifts at the hospital. "It just made work more miserable," Tom said. "I would see Pam not only come home from having a tough day, but then it's like, man, we just can't get out from underneath the debt. That was the ongoing thought. It was just a grind, and you're like, 'Oh, well, just grind through this for the next ten or fifteen years.'"

One day, Pam overheard some colleagues at the hospital remarking on how hot the real estate market was in their area and how hard they were finding it to buy a home. That same day, she suggested to Tom that they put their house on the market. As she pointed out, their three kids were grown and out of the house, so they had more freedom. With interest rates low and sellers wielding overwhelming power, this was their chance to get out of the grind.

Although Tom tended to be a bit more hesitant to make big moves, he was in. If they sold their home for an attractive price, they could pay off all of their debt and lower their financial stress. That in turn would allow them both to work less and to spend more time pursuing their interests.

They called their real estate agent and a couple of weeks later put their house on the market. It sold almost immediately, furniture and all, at $40,000 over their asking price. The next question was: Where would they go? They didn't know. I know that sentence might sound crazy to you. "They sold a house with nowhere to go?" My answer is, "Hell, yeah!" When most people think about real estate transactions, they do the exact opposite: They buy the new place before they sell the existing one. While that might be a gamble worth taking in a hot housing market, it can prove dangerous in a normal or souring market. You could wind up carrying two properties for months, sapping your liquidity. As my father the stock options trader used to say, "I'd rather be short one house than long two!"

Tom and Pam had imagined one day buying a place in Florida or perhaps staying in the Pittsburgh area and downsizing, but they weren't yet prepared to make a decision that might lock them in and limit their future options. Over the short term, the raging housing market in their area would make it very difficult for them to find a house at a reasonable price. So they decided to go on Airbnb and try to find a long-term rental in their local market. And that's where their story gets interesting.

In fairly short order, they found a rental on a horse farm in a rural area within commuting distance of their jobs. It was love at first neigh (I'm so sorry). Pam had been an avid rider growing up; in high school, she'd appeared in horse shows and spent hours caring for and training horses at a local farm. She'd given up the hobby for a time but more recently had picked it up again, leasing a horse at a nearby farm. Now she'd be able to live on a farm that had four horses as well as two donkeys, eight chickens, and two pygmy goats. (Move over, Dr. Doolittle!) The setting was bucolic, with fifteen acres of hiking on the property. At $2,700 a month, the rent would be within their budget, especially since the couple would no longer have all the expenses associated with owning a house to worry about.

Pam and Tom pulled the trigger on the farm, and when I spoke with them in October 2021, they were ecstatic. After selling their house, they had been able to pay off all of their debt and walk away with $250,000 in cash. Their lifestyle became far more relaxed and, frankly, more fun. Although they continued to work, they pared back their hours and filled their days with activities they enjoyed, including exercise, travel, and time with family and friends. Pam spent time each week taking care of animals on the farm, while Tom focused more on his volunteer work. "I wake up with more energy," Pam told me. Being debt-free was "a big burden off." Tom agreed, noting that "it's just phenomenal, a completely different feel." Pam had so much free time now that she began to help out her younger work colleagues by volunteering to watch their kids one day a week so that they could save on childcare expenses. The two still lacked firm plans to buy a new home, but they were thinking through their options and watching the market with the idea of possibly making a purchase when it began to soften.

Many people fear selling their home without a clear endgame in mind. But doing so can allow you to secure *future* opportunity for yourself. When the market is hot, you can benefit from high prices to cash out, pay off debt, and stash money for future endeavors. You can also put yourself in a position to take time away from work to live life, explore, and ponder what's next. If you haven't checked how much equity you have in your home, you might be surprised to find that you finally can break free from a life situation that feels stale, uninspiring, and burdensome. Equity equals choice, but you have to do what Pam and Tom did and move decisively while you have the chance.

Plenty of people sell simply because they see a window to open up future options. One couple in their early sixties, Barb and Rich, had two kids, a son in Texas and a daughter in California. They owned a house in the suburbs worth $1.8 million. They were pretty well situated for retirement; each planned to work part-time for a few years until reaching age sixty-six, when they would claim Social Security benefits.

In 2021, with their local real estate market exploding, Barb and Rich realized that they were sitting on a gold mine that might not be there in years to come if the market soured or even just slowed. Without a particular plan in mind, they sold the house and used a third of the $1.5 million remaining after taxes and fees to buy a small house in Texas, where they wouldn't have to pay state income tax. They figured they could use the balance of the money to fund short-term rentals in California whenever they wanted to visit their daughter. Beyond that, they could bank the money and use it to support themselves over the next seven or eight years. This way, they could wait until age seventy to claim Social Security and qualify for the largest possible retirement benefits, and they wouldn't have to work part-time unless they chose to do so. Pretty amazing, right?

If you're struggling with the idea of selling your cherished home, I feel your pain. But if you hope to undertake a Great Money Reset, there's nothing wrong with a little good, old-fashioned opportunism—your home might be the financial launching pad you need. This is especially true if you can sell while prices are high, but you might possess a surprising amount of equity even in a softer market due to the amount of equity that you've built up over time. Selling earlier than you planned might allow you to do much more with your future: retiring earlier, waiting longer to claim Social Security, enjoying greater flexibility, living closer to your children. Emotions aside, there isn't much of a downside. If you haven't considered selling, I hope you'll at least give it an initial look.

Real Estate as Crisis Management

For some of us, equity in our homes isn't a pathway to opportunity but our ticket out of looming financial catastrophe, a chance to undertake a desperately needed Great Money Reset and finally adopt healthier habits. One of my most memorable on-air phone calls of 2021 came from Alan, a forty-nine-year-old listener from New York City. In the course of introducing himself, Alan remarked that he would put himself "in the 'guy with a lot of financial problems' category." He got that right. Alan and his wife, Marie, were what we financial planner types call the "nearly affluent" or the "working rich." They earned $320,000 a year, quite a nice salary by most standards. Nevertheless, they'd fallen into a horrible cycle of racking up credit card debt and paying it off by refinancing their mortgage or taking a home equity loan. "The stress at this point is pretty close to unbearable for us," Alan said. "And we don't feel like we're living large." When he called me, they were drowning in $110,000 of credit card debt and weren't sure what to do. They were tempted to dip into their $900,000 in retirement savings to pay it off. They also had a $1.3 million apartment to their name, with $400,000 in equity.

Before I could help Alan craft a plan, I had to understand the cause of his family's out-of-control spending. The answer: kids. He and Marie had three of them, ages sixteen, fourteen, and eleven, and they all attended a religious private school. Although the family received financial aid (it's nuts that a family making $320,000 a year qualifies for financial aid, but that's New York City for you), the total tuition bill still ran $35,000 to $40,000 a year—more than the couple's mortgage obligations. In addition, the family had fallen into the trap of what we might call situationally induced spending. Affluent parents at this upscale private school thought nothing of sending their kids to expensive summer camps, paying for an endless array of enrichment activities, taking their families on extravagant vacations, and so on. Although Alan and Marie couldn't afford any of these extras, they felt pressured to provide at least some of them. In recent years, for instance, Alan's kids had attended summer camp—a "massive expense," he said, amounting to over $20,000 for the summer.

I don't like to play the role of Debbie Downer, but I leveled with Alan: He and Marie were in big trouble. With high interest rates, that credit card debt was a ticking time bomb. And if either of them lost their job or experienced some other setback, it could be catastrophic for the family. They needed to make some serious changes—and fast. Refinancing yet again wasn't a viable option. I feared that they would soon wind up facing massive debt once more, this time with little if any equity on which to draw. They also would do well not to pull money from their retirement accounts. Since Alan and Marie were not yet fifty-nine and a half years old, they would have to pay a penalty of 10 percent of the withdrawal amount. They'd also have to pay taxes on the money withdrawn.

Alan and Marie might have been able to borrow against their retirement savings, but if either of them lost their job before repaying the money, they'd face these same penalties and taxes, as the government would consider the outstanding loan amount as an early withdrawal. Ultimately, I feared that if the couple somehow tapped their retirement accounts, they would not break the cycle of excessive spending. For that, they had to take a more dramatic step.

I advised Alan and his wife to pull their kids from private school and send them to public school. Recognizing that they weren't likely to take that step, I pushed them to consider the next best thing: sell their apartment and rent a cheaper one elsewhere. With the proceeds from the sale, they could pay off their credit card debt, establish an emergency fund of at least $100,000, and perhaps prepay some of the private school tuition. Meanwhile, as part of the transition, they would have to sit down together, track every last penny of their monthly expenses, and develop a sound monthly budget.

In addition, Alan and his wife had to level with their kids, informing them as compassionately as possible that the family had to make big changes to their lifestyle to secure its financial foundation. While I am not a fan of saddling your kids with your money issues, when we are talking about a big move that will impact everyone's lives, it is better to be honest. Alan and Marie would do well to explain the game plan to their kids and why it makes sense. A large aspect of their plan was to cop to the fact that in addition to downsizing, they would not be able to pay for college. This is often a tough but necessary admission for parents to make. Having these conversations when the kids enter high school allows them to adjust to reality and make better choices about college.

In addition to making big changes with housing and taking a hatchet to the budget, Alan and Marie needed to reduce their retirement contributions each year to help ensure that they could cover their monthly expense without falling into debt. If the two took these steps, they would stabilize their finances once and for all and alleviate the terrible stress they were feeling.

I wasn't sure if Alan and Marie would take my advice—what I was asking wasn't easy. When I followed up with them in October 2021, I learned that they had recently listed their apartment for sale and were planning to move. Unfortunately, the market had softened, and there was a chance they would get less for it than expected, only $1–$1.2 million. Although selling at that price would leave them with less for an emergency fund and their other needs, I still thought they should go through with it. They would likely save money on housing expenses, but more importantly, making such a big change would create a sense of urgency, increasing the likelihood that the couple would make the tougher changes to their spending habits that were required. I was nervous, though. The couple had used their equity as an emergency escape hatch. If they didn't begin spending within their means now, they would find themselves out of options the next time. As it turned out,

Alan and Marie were able to sell their apartment in late 2021 for over $1.3 million—enough for them to fund a new start.

If you're in a tough spot financially, leveraging the equity you hold in your home might be the way to make it work. But don't undertake this step lightly. Before you sell, confirm there truly are no other viable options, and commit yourself to making any other changes that might be necessary to render your financial life more sustainable. For many of us, selling our homes represents our final chance to stay solvent and prevent our financial lives from caving in on us. It's a big risk, but one that might help us change unhealthy patterns and stabilize our situation going forward.

Rethinking the Real Estate Rules

Besides the emotional attachment we might have to an existing property, many of us fail to take advantage of our equity to fund a Great Money Reset because we're scared. A home is such a big asset, and we don't want to do anything that we'll regret later. To justify our inaction, we point to any number of real estate "rules" that might suggest that buying or selling is a bad idea. Other rules out there can have the opposite effect, prompting us to leap too quickly into buying or selling a home even when it's not in our interest. I'm here to tell you that at least some of these rules either are outdated or might not apply to you. Let's take a look.

Rule #1: If You're Selling Your Home and Buying a New One, It's Advantageous to Buy a Fixer-Upper

As the experts have long opined, you'll generate more long-term value for yourself if you buy a house and fix it up than you will by buying one that's already been rehabbed. That once made sense, but it's not clear that it still does. During the pandemic, the cost of raw materials and labor caused the price of renovations to skyrocket. In one case I know of, neighbors of mine got a $600,000 estimate for a project they were planning. They never pulled the trigger, and two years later when they again asked for bids that same project cost $1.4 million. I know, crazy. Supply chain issues also forced homeowners to wait months for appliances, furniture, and other goods—when they could get them at all.

Maybe you can still find a fixer-upper that represents a good financial deal in your local market. But don't pass up properties that are in better shape simply because that seems like a wise thing to do. It might not be. Inflationary pressures aside, perhaps you're just not the kind of person with the time or interest to see an extensive renovation through. In that case, buying a newer property might save you a ton of stress, not to mention money.

Rule #2: *You're Foolish to Sell When Real Estate Prices Are Falling*

Um, not necessarily. One young couple I know lived in a tiny studio apartment in Chicago. They were yearning to upgrade to a larger two-bedroom. Just as they were starting to pay attention to the market, COVID-19 struck, an exodus from metropolitan areas took place, and prices in Chicago and other big cities fell. This couple was upset, convinced that they'd lost their opportunity to sell for the foreseeable future—their sale price would be much lower than it would have been just a year earlier. What they weren't considering was that the price of the two-bedroom would be lower, too. In their case, selling and buying a new home still made sense.

Don't talk yourself out of making a Great Money Reset just because prices have fallen. When you're assessing the real estate market, you really do need to look at both sides of it. If you already own a property, shifts either way in the market might work out to be a wash for you.

Rule #3: *If Renting Is Cheaper than Buying, Then You Should Do That*

I have long been a fan of renting—if you don't believe me, go back and read my first book. The fact is that many of us *are* overly eager to jump into owning a house, underestimating the financial burden as well as how easy it might be to sell if our circumstances change. Since the pandemic, however, shifts in the market make the financial benefits of renting a bit less clear. In periods of high inflation such as this, renters might get hit with annual rent increases that are bigger than they anticipated. By buying or signing a longer-term lease, they might be better able to achieve stability in their housing costs.

Meanwhile, one of the big benefits that renting confers— flexibility—might not be as attractive as it once was. Prior to the pandemic, many people needed to keep their options open, not knowing if they'd have to relocate suddenly for work in a year or two. Today, however, many white-collar professionals can work remotely—a trend that is poised to continue or even intensify. If you enjoy such a work situation, you might hesitate less to pony up a down payment, knowing that you might not have to move as often or at all as your career advances.

This is not to say that buying necessarily represents a better choice for you. It comes down to your specific situation. For instance, many people who think about buying simultaneously contemplate a move out of expensive cities and into cheaper suburbs, where ownership is more affordable. If you fall into this camp, then you'll also want to consider whether you really can stomach life in the suburbs. Many of the urban dwellers who fled major metropolitan areas during the pandemic's early days have flocked back. Although the quiet and safety of suburban life sounded great, they wound up missing the excitement and energy that urban life has to offer. Even if you can afford to buy in a suburb, renting in a city might be a more realistic option for you, one that will leave you happier and better off over the long term.

When it comes to renting or buying, you can't approach it as simply a financial decision. And even the financial piece of it might be murkier than it once was. Think through this decision carefully, evaluating your specific circumstances to determine the best course of action. If you can't afford to own or you really don't know what kind of living situation you want, then strongly consider renting. Otherwise, you still might want to rent, but be aware that buying can also allow you the peace of mind of knowing with some precision what the majority of your housing costs will be in the years ahead.

Rule #4: Moving to a Cheaper Locale Is a Smart Move

It can be, but not necessarily. If you're moving to take advantage of a cheaper cost of living or lower tax rates, that's great. But again, many people underestimate the emotional costs of such a move. Do you really *want* to live in this new location? If not, you might be setting yourself up for a world of pain, which is definitely not what a Great Money Reset is supposed to be about.

When contemplating a change of scenery, ask yourself whether it really will make you happy. Also, consider other factors that might be influencing your choice. If you're also moving to be closer to your kids, do you know for certain that they're going to stick around? If you're excited about the recreational activities available in the area, will those really be enough for you?

One couple I know in their fifties rented a condo for a month in Santa Fe, New Mexico. Residents of New Hampshire, they were looking for a place to spend the harsh winter months in the years to come and had heard wonderful things about Santa Fe. Their plan was to rent this year as a prelude to buying a condo. Although they had assumed that Santa Fe would be more affordable than living in a northeastern city, after just a month they were surprised to find out how much *less* housing they could get for their money. Also, although they liked Santa Fe itself, they felt that the town was fairly isolated and lacked access to other big cities and the amenities they offered. If they had been avid outdoorspeople, Santa Fe might have been perfect for them. Since they weren't, this location wouldn't satisfy their desires. They resolved to look at other warm-weather locales both in the United States and abroad.

I always get nervous when people announce their intention to move. Maybe they're making a sound decision, but I worry that they might not know what they're getting themselves into. Do your research. Look beyond the finances. And if you can, visit the place to which you are planning to move and test it out.

Rule #5: If the Market Is Hot and You Have Any Inclination to Sell, Do It

I know I extolled the merits of acting opportunistically, but you'd be foolish to take it too far. At the height of the pandemic, as real estate prices shot up nationwide, one resident of a tony Chicago suburb decided to sell his multimillion-dollar home. This gentleman, in his great wisdom, was convinced that the global economy was on the verge of collapse. Home prices would never again be as high, he thought, so it was time for him to sell and lock in his gains. He did so and moved to a rental, only to find that housing prices rose even further the following year. When I last heard, this gentleman desperately wanted to buy another home but was reluctant to do so, as he would be locking in a loss. For the time being, he was stuck, not to mention embarrassed. As a friend of his noted, his housing situation had become "a very sore subject."

A hot market isn't necessarily a license to sell. Timing the market is always a dicey proposition. Some people attempt to do it and come out ahead. Others make the mistake of a lifetime. Again, look beyond the financial dimensions. Make sure the move you're contemplating really will make you happy. The people we've highlighted in this chapter all sold because it made financial sense. But all of them made darn sure they wanted to live in their new locale. And when they didn't know exactly what they wanted to do next, they left options open for themselves.

It's About *You*

There's a broader point here. When considering a real estate move as part of a Great Money Reset, try to tune out all the other people in your life who might be telling you what to do, whether it's your parents, your children, your friends, or even well-meaning experts such as myself. Instead, think for yourself, clarifying what will make your life better, happier, and more fulfilled as you define those terms.

One couple, Beth and Irma, had a lovely weekend house right on the beach within driving distance of a major metropolitan area. They learned that the property adjacent to theirs was on the market. Their first inclination was to snap it up. They loved their location and feared that a buyer might come along, tear down the quaint little beach cottages that now stood on this land, and build a McMansion next to their smaller bungalow. Or perhaps this buyer would keep the cottages and turn them into Airbnb rentals, with strangers constantly coming and going.

Friends and neighbors urged Beth and Irma to buy the property—the two would be crazy not to, they said. So the couple contacted a friend who was a builder and asked him what he thought they should pay for it. His advice: If they could get the property for $1 million, it would be a steal. Fair market value was probably $1.4–$1.5 million. Armed with this knowledge, Beth and Irma approached the owner and asked what he would accept for it. The answer: $2.2 million.

Although this was well beyond what appeared to be fair market value, the two were ready to plunk down the money anyway, so influenced were they by those around them. They imagined all that they would do with the land—the gardens they'd create, more room for their dogs to play.

Fortunately, they happened to chat with a relative who had a sharp financial mind. "Are you crazy?" he asked. "You must have much more money than I think, because you're telling me that you're ready to pay $2 million for a bigger yard. That's bonkers." For the first time, Beth and Irma heard a dissenting opinion, and it shook them out of buying mode. They knew that this guy was right.

They passed on the deal, hoping that whoever bought the property wouldn't ruin their private little paradise. It turned out that they were right not to buy. The property quickly sold, and the new buyer decided that he would keep it just as it was. "I could not have been in a better situation," my friend told me. "We actually feel like we made $2 million because we didn't spend money on this thing, there is no McMansion or Airbnb rental, and we have a wonderful neighbor."

We can't put too much store in what others tell us, not least because of the role luck often plays in life. Others around us might be right, but they might be wrong, too. The wisest moves we can make are usually those that come from someplace deeper inside us. That way, we'll feel calm and resolved in our choices no matter how situations work out. When it came down to it, Beth and Irma didn't really feel comfortable putting $2 million into a bigger backyard. It just wasn't right for them. They passed on the deal, knowing that they'd chosen wisely. As an added bonus, they now have more funds at their disposal to undertake another Great Money Reset someday, one that might prove far more consequential and meaningful.

Sure, pay some attention to other voices, but get in touch with yourself before making your final decision. Become quiet and introspective and think through the particulars of a situation, what it might mean for you, and how you really feel about it. And make real estate part of your deliberations. Your home may be your biggest asset, so it will likely be a key part of any plans you might make for your future. You might feel emotionally connected to your home and reluctant to part with it, but if you're thinking of shaking up your life, or if you desperately need to do so, you might have more to gain from a sale than you ever imagined.

Rock the Reset

- Rising real estate values can make possible a Great Money Reset that might otherwise have proven elusive. But first get real about fears and attachments you might have that prompt you to hold on too long or delay a purchase.

- Although selling your home without a clear endgame in mind can be scary, doing so may allow you to secure *future* opportunity for yourself.

- Real estate might be your ticket out of looming financial catastrophe, but make sure first that other options aren't open to you and that you're willing to change the underlying habits that got you into trouble in the first place.

- Some conventional wisdom about real estate might be out of date. When making decisions, don't focus too much on "the rules of thumb" or on what others say. Think primarily about what *you* want and need.

7

Start, Sell, or Evolve
a Business

Do you want to spend the next twenty years toiling away for someone else, or is it time to go it alone? Whether it's starting a new business, developing a side hustle, or cashing out, don't let a good crisis go to waste!

Have you ever had a hands-down *brilliant* idea for a new business that you didn't develop, only to find that someone else did and was making a fortune? If so, Cheri Ruane, a landscape architect in Boston, knows your pain. During the 1990s, when she was killing herself each day trying to squeeze her car into the city's tiny urban parking spaces, she had a revelation of sorts. What if she were to invent a simple device that you could store in your trunk and then attach to your bumper to protect it—a kind of bumper for your bumper?

Cheri started to work on the concept, creating a mock-up from materials she bought at Home Depot. Unfortunately, her efforts stalled. She got distracted by her day job and her growing family and forgot all about "the Bumper," as she called her product. Two years later, she saw that someone else had successfully marketed a very similar idea—they called it the Bumper Bully. *Dang it,* she thought. *Why didn't I see that through?*

Ruane has let other good business ideas come and go. She just didn't have the time, determination, or fire to see them to fruition. But in 2020, when the pandemic hit, she resolved finally to take entrepreneurialism more seriously. Bored and looking for an outlet, she first had an idea to create a business making homemade masks in her spare time and selling them on Etsy. After digging up an old sewing machine from her basement and watching a few YouTube instructional videos, she got busy designing masks. Her products were beautiful, and within a year she had sold about $20,000 worth of them. Since she had continued to work full-time, that income amounted to a small windfall. Cheri put it to proper use, donating some of it to a nonprofit girls' camp, contributing to the capital campaign at her rowing club, and taking her family on vacation.

She might have continued her mask-making endeavors had she not come up with an idea that was *even cooler.* Cheri and her husband had separated a few years earlier. To help distract herself during the pandemic, she immersed herself in the wacky world (some might say bottomless pit) of online dating. Before long, she was meeting people on several dating apps and became, in her words, an "active dater."[1] But she quickly noticed a problem: Dating online was pretty taxing on the brain.

On each of the dating sites Cheri frequented, she was flirting at any given time with two or three people. She would often take conversations that began on dating sites onto other digital communication sites such as Kick, Snapchat, WhatsApp, and Signal. All told, she might have had eighteen to twenty conversations going at once with eight or nine people across the various platforms, with old love interests drifting away and new ones popping up. How could she keep it all straight? Cheri found that she forgot details about people she met online, making for some awkward moments. In one instance, she asked one of her love interests what he did for a living. He was a dentist and tartly remarked that he had already told her that three times (ouch, hard to rinse that one out).

A dating guru might have advised Cheri to try a simple life hack: *Slow it down.* But Cheri didn't want to. She was having great fun, meeting an array of interesting people and learning about their lives. Instead, she began keeping better track of her activity, jotting down notes about her dating contacts in a special journal. As the journal had a black cover, she began to joke that she was keeping a "little black book," as swinging

1 Cheri Ruane, interview with the author, January 12, 2022.

singles in previous generations had done. And then it dawned on her: There should be an app for this.

She quickly determined that no app like this was currently on the market. Cheri wasn't about to let another great business idea get away, so she started a new online business, a dating organizer app called Bl@ckbook. Once again, she continued to work at her full-time job—this would be a strictly off-hours venture. She began to conduct research, speak to professional matchmakers and dating coaches, and learn how to start an online business.

To fund her start-up, she drained $10,000 from a special fund she had created years earlier to pay for a future facelift. "I'm slightly vain," Cheri explained, "and just knew that at some point I was going to want a facelift, so I started saving." We all should create a self-care fund for a rainy day, don't you think?

In any case, Cheri used the money to hire developers, create the app, and pay for some initial marketing. In October 2021, Bl@ckbook went live. Cheri's goal was to build up a user base of 100,000 or more for the app, prove that it was a viable business, and then sell it to one of the big online dating companies. She hoped to earn a decent payday from her efforts—who knows, maybe even a life-changing one.

When I spoke to Cheri a couple of months into her new venture, the app hadn't yet taken off—she had logged only about five hundred downloads. But she was working hard to help it to go viral in the United States and several other countries. She was also looking at other potential uses for the technology, such as helping fundraisers track their leads or new moms keep track of playdates. Still, dating seemed to be the most promising application. "As I've discovered, there really is no competition for this product in the dating space. It doesn't exist. So either it's genius or it's the stupidest idea ever. I guess we'll find out."

I think it's a unique idea with great potential, and I hope for Cheri's sake that the world agrees. I also hope that you'll feel inspired by Cheri's story to pay heed to that little voice inside your head that might be telling you to start your own business. Times of personal difficulty often are just what we need to get our entrepreneurial juices flowing. As painful as it can be, chaos can break us free of long-standing assumptions and allow us to see the world afresh. As we struggle with our own difficulties, we might wonder aloud why a solution doesn't exist. And with less to lose, we might feel emboldened to build that solution ourselves and market it to others. When the world is going to pot, why *not* make a bet on ourselves?

Word to the Wise: Make It a Small Bet

Cheri's story and others I've encountered point us to an important rule of the road: *Start slow.* Cheri didn't blow up her existing life just because she had a nifty business idea. Since she had energy to burn and was willing to hustle during her spare time, she could keep her current job and enjoy the stability and peace of mind it afforded. She didn't hate her job and wasn't seeking a big career change. She simply liked the challenge of getting a successful business off the ground and welcomed a potentially big payday if she could succeed.

A business idea you have might excite you, but don't get carried away. Rather than rush into an entrepreneurial venture, you might do well to gain relevant experience or knowledge first by taking it on as a side hustle. Chris Guillebeau, author of the book *Side Hustle*, posits that most normal human beings don't wish to be hard-core entrepreneurs.[2] They just want to round out their lives by pursuing passions and interests on the side to earn extra money. But let's say you do harbor entrepreneurial dreams. You can often test-drive these dreams and make some bank by doing an initial project or gig. If you dream of starting your own marketing communications firm, look for a chance to help a company write some newsletters or social media posts. If you dream of opening a bakery, start by baking cakes for the holidays and marketing them to friends and family.

My friend Andrea Meyerson took this approach, and it paid off. By the mid-1990s, she had built up a successful and quite lucrative career in corporate America. But after coming out as a lesbian, she sensed that gay women didn't have many options to socialize and have fun together outside of the bar scene. Should she quit her job and start a company that put on social events for lesbians? Not so fast. Since she

---

2 Chris Guillebeau, *Side Hustle: From Idea to Income in 27 Days* (London: Macmillan, 2017).

was an avid cyclist, Andrea started a lesbian bicycling club called Women on a Roll and organized events. It was a side hustle, something fun to do during her off-hours.

The club quickly became popular, and Andrea found herself organizing parties that attracted hundreds of women. After about two years, she began producing live fundraising events (concerts, sporting events, and so on) targeted at the lesbian community through a company she started, StandOut Productions. She also developed a travel business through Women on a Roll, organizing women-only group trips around the world. At each destination, Andrea curated special experiences on the ground, finding local guides who were happy to cater to gay women.

Only when she began producing fundraising events did Andrea quit her corporate job. She had always thought she would be crazy to leave the corporate world—the salary and perks were just too good, she liked the work, and her job afforded her considerable autonomy. But in serving the lesbian community, she had found something many of us crave: a sense of purpose. What had started as a side hustle soon became much more than that—a second career and her life's calling. By starting small, she had minimized her risk, confirming that a need existed in the lesbian community for a social organizer and realizing that she enjoyed filling this role.

If you start with a side hustle, you might see the need to invest some seed money. Here again, tread softly. Make sure you commit only an amount of money that you'd feel comfortable losing if your business venture failed within a year.

Your objective should be to test whether your venture could be self-sustaining—if not right now, then at some point in the future. Cheri didn't tap into her retirement savings or take out a second mortgage to start Bl@ckbook. All she risked was some facelift money. If she lost it, she'd still have a roof over her head, food on her table, and a comfortable retirement in her future.

As you test your idea, pay close attention to how you feel about it. Although our culture glamorizes the entrepreneurial life, it isn't for everyone. Spencer Brown, a serial entrepreneur and radio executive, believes that a lack of honest reflection is one of the biggest mistakes would-be entrepreneurs make. Entrepreneurialism "sounds great," he told me. "I'm going to work for myself. I'm going to set my own hours. I'm not going to have a boss."[3] But there's another side to it: responsibility. The success of your venture is all on you. You're the one who must do the grunt work. You're the one who must get out there to drum up business. You're the one who must make the tough decisions. Can you handle the pressure? As Spencer noted, "The excitement of running your own business quickly matures into reality, and a lot of people aren't ready for it."

Before jumping with both feet into a new venture, ask whether you can really see yourself doing it full-time. Do you like working for yourself as much as you thought? What would it take to make the business all it could be? If your

---

3 Spencer Brown, interview with the author, January 28, 2022.

new venture isn't compelling enough to justify quitting your current job, might it still make sense to keep your side hustle going, whether as a hobby or as a kind of insurance policy should you ever lose that job?

Spencer also recommends asking a slew of practical questions: Are you in a financial position to work without a salary for a certain period of time? How much capital will you ultimately need? How long will it take before you turn a profit? What will it take not merely to start the business, but to manage and grow it? Do you have the financial wherewithal so that you won't be terrified at every turn of going bankrupt? He and other entrepreneurs I know suggest sketching out a brief business plan, including an income statement for the first couple of years. For a reality check, you might also turn to a trusted advisor or mentor.

You can also minimize your risk by lowering your overhead. When Andrea started as an entrepreneur, she decided to live simply and cheaply to minimize the stress of generating income. She continues that practice today, renting out part of her house to help cover the mortgage and keeping a tight rein on her spending. "I don't make a ton of money, but I'm not hurting," she said. "I live nicely without a lot of stress because I've decided to keep my overhead as low as possible."

We tend to think of entrepreneurs as inveterate risk-takers, and there's truth to that stereotype. But most successful entrepreneurs I know give serious thought to moderating their risk upon starting new ventures. Spencer is a case in point. He started his career as a commercial litigator working for a big New York law firm. After realizing that all those dusty law books just weren't for him, he took *seven years* to transition into a career as an entrepreneur. First he got his M.B.A. Then he gained practical business experience by working for several years for his father's boutique investment bank. Just as he was getting antsy in that role, an entrepreneurial opportunity presented itself. "That's another piece of advice I'd give to people," he said. Don't rush into entrepreneurialism. "You've got to pick the right time and circumstance" to make the leap.[4] Spencer was willing to work patiently to gain the knowledge and experience he'd eventually need to succeed. For him, going off on his own was a risk, but a smart, measured one. It should be the same for you.

The Freelance Hustle

Andrea and Spencer both started new ventures that bore little relation to their previous professional roles. For some of us, entrepreneurialism might entail keeping those roles intact but operating on a contract or freelance basis instead of as a full-time employee. This, too, is an important option to consider when thinking about making a Great Money Reset.

If you're nearing retirement, working as a freelancer might serve you well as a way of transitioning slowly away from your

---

4 Spencer Brown, interview with the author, January 28, 2022.

professional career. If you love what you do, you can still do it, only without the pressures and time commitment that come with full-time employment. For younger workers, becoming a contractor can afford you many advantages, including more flexibility and autonomy, more varied work, and perhaps the chance to earn a higher income.

It's important to understand the downsides that come with self-employment, especially if you're younger. Although you might be able to charge a higher rate, you usually will have to pony up for your own benefits, including healthcare and retirement (alas, no more employer match). Although you can tap some attractive tax benefits (see Chapter 5), you also have to pay federal payroll taxes both as an employer and as an employee.

A bigger challenge that many people confront upon becoming a contractor is the lack of job security. As an employee, you can rely on a paycheck coming your way each month. Not so as a freelancer. Business from existing clients can dry up for all kinds of reasons, including business downturns, the departure of your client from their company, changing strategic priorities at your client's company, and other factors beyond your control. Cash flow issues can also crop up: You might bill a client in February, but they might not pay you until June. In the meantime, you must still cover your monthly expenses. Are you ready for the stress of constantly hustling for new clients and chasing down existing ones who owe you money? Do you have enough funds saved to weather periods of slower business? Do you have a strong enough network to allow for a steady stream of work?

The same advice offered previously applies here: Start slow. You might want to wait until you have at least one good, "anchor" client locked in before transitioning full-time to contract work. When I made my own Great Money Reset, selling my interest in my financial planning firm and becoming an on-air financial expert, I was hired as an employee at CBS's Interactive division to help launch the network's Moneywatch.com site. After a couple of years, I found that I loved my work but missed the entrepreneurial spirit that had allowed me to grow my former company. I longed to create opportunities inside CBS, but I also wanted the freedom to pursue cool projects outside of the organization.

I decided to call it quits as an employee and perform the same work on a contract basis. But I only made this big move after executives at CBS News committed to hiring me as a freelancer to appear on radio and local and national television. This contract alone wouldn't suffice to cover all of my bills, but it would serve as a great anchor for me to establish a successful business. With CBS locked in as a client, I knew I would have a certain amount of monthly revenue. Since I liked to sell and was good at it, I thought I would likely build on this contract and generate a good income overall. If I hadn't had CBS on board, I probably would have remained an employee. Going off on my own would have felt too scary.

To find an anchor client, you might need to think more broadly about the kinds of projects you're willing to take on. One friend of mine left a full-time job as a consumer researcher and analyst at an advertising agency with the idea of setting himself up as a freelance writer. He managed to get some work right away, but not enough to fully cover his expenses. To add to his income and ensure a bit of stability, he signed a year-long, renewable contract to work on a part-time basis with a different advertising agency as a researcher. The work wasn't what he desired, but the pay was great, amounting to almost half of what he hoped to make each year, so the contract worked as a temporary solution. My friend wound up maintaining this contract for several years. By the time it ended, he had built his writing business up to the point where he could replace the lost income without much trouble.

If it's possible to lock in longer-term contracts up front, do it, even if the work isn't exactly what you seek. If you can find ways to minimize your expenses at first (for instance, by working out of your home, or doing without an assistant or other support staff), do that, too. And if you can find a reliable source of new business (for instance, by allying yourself with an influencer in your field), all the better. Working freelance can be extremely rewarding, but only if you can handle the uncertainty and instability that often come with it.

The $7 Million Man

Readers of a certain age will remember the classic 1970s television show *The Six Million Dollar Man*. Well, I was honored in 2021 to receive an on-air call from a $7 million man. Brent hailed from Colorado, and he wanted advice about how to sell a software business he and two partners had started a decade earlier.

I found Brent's situation fascinating. At age forty, he had been married for sixteen years and had eight kids—yes, eight!—ages seven months to fifteen years. As he noted, he would have kids in college, and the bills associated with them, for a full twenty-year period. Thank goodness he had his business. Although he was drawing only about $225,000 annually in salary and bonuses, his company had grown considerably during the pandemic and was now worth about $22 million. If he and his partners sold, each would walk away with a bit over $7 million. After taxes, that might mean a $5 million pay-day for Brent. He hoped to set aside a portion of that money for college educations and use the rest of it to fund his other needs, including a bigger living space (believe it or not, this family of ten was living in a 2,200-square-foot house). Like many entrepreneurs, Brent hadn't managed to save much for the future. He had only $125,000 socked away for retirement and a meager emergency fund of $20,000, so those areas would need some TLC as well.

When I asked Brent why he wanted to sell the business right now, he told me that he and his partners just thought that the time was right. Given how hyped up the financial markets were, he thought their business would fetch a good price. Brent also felt strongly about taking some financial risk off the table. At this point, his stake in the business represented the vast majority of his net worth (he owned a home worth about $800,000). He didn't know if the economy would fizzle sometime soon, causing his business to dry up, or if a competitor would come along and steal away clients. It was a safer bet, he thought, to cash out while he could. Brent wasn't looking to become the next Bill Gates or retire to a life of endless golf. He liked what he did and hoped to continue working for the company under its new owners. He just wanted the peace of mind that would come from a sale that would transform his share of the business into a liquid asset.

For established entrepreneurs, a Great Money Reset might involve selling an existing company, not starting a new one. Brent's story suggests an important rule of thumb, which is that if you're going to do it, don't let greed get the better of you. Many entrepreneurs focus on one consideration above others when pondering a sale: getting the highest price. They think that if they wait, a business that today is worth $5 million might become a bonanza worth $10 million, $15 million, or more. They don't want to be that "sucker" who sold "too early." Such logic often backfires. In waiting for a bigger payday, many entrepreneurs find they've waited too long, and that beautiful little company they started and lovingly built has declined in value.

As a company founder, I like a fat sales price as much as anyone. The last thing I'd want an entrepreneur to do after pumping their blood, sweat, and tears into an enterprise for years on end is to forgo a big portion of the value they created. But mitigating risk matters, too. Brent was right to want to take some cash off the table, especially since he had so many mouths to feed. If he was sure that he and his partners could grow the business appreciably within a few short years, that might have changed the calculation. Since he wasn't, he was probably smart to push for a sale while demand for his company's products was strong and the market for companies like his was hot.

If you're thinking of selling a business, would the proceeds from its sale in its present state be life-changing for you? If so, you might want to sell now and take some of that big, risky bet off the table. That's doubly true if, like Brent, you've been underpaying yourself all along and thus shorting yourself of some of the value you helped create. But there are other questions to ask: Can you realistically grow the business further, or have you taken it as far as you can? Do economic and consumer trends favor future growth, or are those trends currently at their peak?

You should also look inward to probe your own feelings about your business. How much do you really enjoy running it day to day? Are you ready for something new in your life, or are you so emotionally attached to the business that it would be tough to let it go? What might bother you more in the future: the possibility that you could have sold the business for more, or the fact that you tried for a bigger payday and missed your chance to sell? If you did sell now, would you constantly look back at the decision, pondering whether it was right, or would you quickly move on?

For many entrepreneurs, removing risk through a sale can prove quite satisfying. Spencer Brown, the radio entrepreneur, had successfully sold a previous company before founding the podcast company Cadence 13 in 2015. This company grew rapidly as podcasting became popular as a communications channel. Within a few years, though, Spencer concluded it was time to sell. "Being honest with myself, we got to the point where it would have taken a lot more capital than we had to get where I thought we needed to go."

Could Spencer and his partners have stuck it out for a couple more years in hopes of obtaining a higher sale price? Perhaps. But it seemed smart to take liquidity out of the business. For Spencer personally, it would be a relief to cash out and provide for his family's financial future, especially since he wasn't getting any younger (he was in his mid-fifties). In 2019, when the right buyer came along, Spencer and his partners did a deal. "I don't second-guess the decision," he told me. "I think it was a good moment to exit." Spencer has since launched a new venture and is excited for his next chapter.

It's not crazy to stick with a business longer in search of greater gains. Just know that you don't have to—there's no shame in trading some of that potential value for less risk. We tend to hear about all the billion-dollar sales that worked out because entrepreneurs grew their businesses to a certain point and then sold. We don't hear so much about entrepreneurs who tried to grow to a billion dollars but failed, often for reasons unrelated to their own performance. If you have the opportunity to sell now and make a major money reset, I would urge you to at least entertain the possibility.

Evolve or Die

"Okay, Jill," you say, "let's say I *did* wait too long, and my company is now on a swift decline. What do I do? More generally, what do I do if the winds of change have turned against my business and I find myself unexpectedly with products and services nobody wishes to buy?"

Here again, you're looking at a major money reset, one that most of us would prefer to avoid. You might presume that your best course of action is to sell or shut down your business, lick your wounds, and move on. Not necessarily. There might be another opportunity to consider, one that sometimes eludes entrepreneurs: *evolve*.

Remember my friend Andrea, the one who built a career producing fundraising events and travel experiences for the lesbian community? In February 2020, her company Women on a Roll had just concluded a successful trip to Thailand and she was looking forward to a busy year that would include the company's twenty-fifth-anniversary gala, a trip to New Orleans, a concert event featuring Brandi Carlile, and a trip to Italy. Just weeks later, however, COVID struck, forcing Andrea to cancel all of these events. She was devastated. "I'm not a person who gets depressed," she said, "but I was looking at the world shutting down and thinking, *What in the hell am I going to do?*"

As a longtime entrepreneur, Andrea was used to improvising when life didn't go according to plan, and she did so in this case as well. She thought carefully about potential opportunities she hadn't noticed before. What did her core customer base—members of the lesbian community—need at this point? One day she heard of a videoconferencing service called Zoom that some in corporate America were just discovering. Googling "Zoom," she wondered whether she might produce gatherings on this platform instead of at in-person venues. Like most everyone else, gay women were stuck at home, deprived of fun social and cultural experiences. Perhaps virtual events could fill that gaping hole that had suddenly opened in their lives.

Andrea called a colleague of hers who handled technology for her business and told him about her idea. He thought it was amazing and helped her set up a Zoom account. Attending webinars offered by the company, she learned everything she needed to know about holding events using the service. She began to contact the performers she had worked with in her live productions and asked if they'd be willing to appear on the Zoom events she was organizing. As their tours and live appearances had also come to a halt, they were very willing to give it a try, viewing it as an opportunity to stay connected with their fan base. It turned out that these online offerings not only served Andrea's customers but entertainers as well.

Within a week, Andrea launched her new service of online entertainment, initially offering Zoom performances to her existing customer base for free with a virtual tip jar for performers. Before long, the service blew up. Andrea was producing three shows a night, five nights a week, for up to a hundred viewers, the maximum that Andrea's Zoom account could accommodate at the time. Five months into it, she relaunched the business as a subscription service called Women on the Net, with customers paying for unlimited access to the Zoom shows (you could pay per show as well if you liked). She also increased her Zoom account capacity to be able to host up to three hundred people at each event.

The service was a big success, profitable within two months. When I spoke with Andrea in January 2022, she had hosted over five hundred events featuring top talent—musical acts like the Indigo Girls and Sophie B. Hawkins, actresses like Lily Tomlin and Meredith Baxter, comedians like Paula Poundstone and Kate Clinton, athletes like Martina Navratilova and Billie Jean King, public figures like Karine Jean-Pierre, and many others. In addition to these shows, Women on the Net hosted a range of social events—films with talkbacks, themed parties, panels, game shows, singles events, dance classes, meditation sessions—all held virtually.

Women on the Net has been a godsend for Andrea, and not just financially. She found a powerful new way to serve her community, one that revitalized her sense of purpose. During the pandemic, the traditional places where gay women met one another and socialized, including bookstores and bars, withered away. Women on the Net became a vital substitute, bringing together women who now felt quite isolated from one another and lonely. "What happened is really quite magical," she told me. "Women from all over the country and even the world became the best of friends, and they never met in person. They often refer to themselves as the "Women on the Net family." I have received so many cards and letters from people saying what a difference it has made for them." Given this response, Andrea has no plans to scale back Women on the Net as the pandemic fades. "I can do this until the day I die," she said. "I'm in my heaven, creating such fun events and working with such great talent, and dealing with such a wonderful, appreciative community. It's very fulfilling."

In the midst of her initial doldrums, Andrea might have shut down her travel and live-events business, but she didn't. After allowing herself a short period to reflect and worry, she set about *evolving* her business, taking it in an unexpected and delightful direction. She didn't risk much in order to do so, either. She mustered her existing assets, most notably her network of great talent, made small investments in technology, and experimented by offering a free service. Only when she established that demand existed for her service did she turn it into a viable business. She was also well placed to make this pivot in part because she had been a disciplined spender all along, keeping her overhead low.

If you find your existing business struggling, whether because of a pandemic, a market downturn, or some other setback, tap into your latent capacity for resilience. Although some of us are built tougher than others, we all have some ability to adapt and adjust to changes in circumstances that are beyond our control. Remind yourself of the strengths and resources you have at your disposal, and take comfort in them.

Then try to take a fresh look at the world around you.

Don't just consider the obvious choices at your disposal: selling your business, shutting it down, or plodding ahead as it experiences a slow decline. Try to imagine new opportunities. What might people today want or need that you might viably deliver? What new offerings might you enjoy creating for your existing customer base? Might some creative tweaks to your business model help you to ride out the storm?

Tamara, an entrepreneur and an avid musician, built a small-scale business around a new technology that she created. After spending several years building up a book of sales, Tamara planned to sell the business and either retire or move on to a new project. To her dismay, a series of negotiations with potential buyers fell through—the offers just weren't high enough. Rather than despair, this entrepreneur had an idea: What if she could partner with one of these prospective buyers, a much larger company, instead of selling to them?

Tamara wound up formalizing a partnership whereby the larger company took on responsibility for selling and marketing the product, while she provided the technical expertise required to deliver it to customers. Providing technical expertise didn't require much time or effort, so this arrangement would provide Tamara with the holy grail: a largely passive source of income. In addition, if her partner were to grow sales over the next couple of years, the value of Tamara's company might increase, making it attractive for her to sell down the road.

Although it's still early days, the arrangement seems poised for success. Tamara didn't like sales all that much, but the nature of her product meant a constant pressure to attend trade shows. Getting out there in front of buyers was also expensive, costing up to $50,000 each year in travel and trade show registration fees. Tamara was more than happy to off-load all of this to her partner, which already had a large sales force of its own. The arrangement amounted to an evolution of Tamara's business—an unforeseen shift born out of adversity, and one that made great sense.

There's a more general lesson embedded here. For any of us, a Great Money Reset is really just a chance to evolve our life as opposed to letting it drift, stagnate, and wither. In an act of courage, we venture past our existing, comfortable realities, pursuing possibilities that we believe we'll find more satisfying and energizing, if not more remunerative. Entrepreneurialism can often be the vehicle for this personal evolution, whether it's starting a new business or selling or transforming an existing one. If you're feeling stuck, I invite you to explore these possibilities. More profoundly, I invite you—as I have throughout this book—to unleash a kind of entrepreneurial spirit inside yourself, taking charge of your life, probing your emotions, exploring your options, and taking a series of smart, reasonable, and thoughtful steps toward a better future.

Rock the Reset

- Thinking of starting a business? Chaotic or difficult times are often just what we need to get our entrepreneurial juices flowing.

- Start slowly. Don't blow up your life just because you thought of a cool idea. Begin with a side hustle, which can allow you to learn and work out the kinks.

- If you're nearing retirement age, working as a freelancer may be a way of transitioning away from your professional career. But be prepared to hustle!

- If you're thinking of selling an existing business, don't get greedy and wait too long in hopes of the highest possible price. If you did wait too long and your business is now struggling, tap into your latent capacity for resilience and try to evolve your business.

8

Educate Yourself

Would it help to upgrade your skills to make a leap forward? Is a graduate degree worth it, or would a certificate program deliver a better return on your time and money? Before you plunk down a single dollar, read this chapter.

In March 2020, as COVID was taking hold and the country was poised to enter lockdown, my partner and I enjoyed what would become a final weekend of normalcy at our vacation home, hosting our dear friend's son Jimmy and his new wife. Scarcely had we sat down to dinner when Jimmy threw some news our way that sent me into shock: He was quitting his job paying about $75,000 a year to go back to school to get a certification in computer coding.

Now, I have nothing against coding. But in Jimmy's case, quitting a reasonably well-paying job to program computers seemed like the height of folly. Jimmy hadn't naturally gravitated toward tech—he'd always been more of a humanities guy. In fact, his mother had always believed he would become a great fiction writer. Coding seemed like a career detour, a way of putting off adult responsibility. Since graduating from college in 2015 with a degree in metropolitan studies (an interdisciplinary approach to the rise of cities, which, according to Jimmy, "is kind of like urban planning, but a little mushier and a lot less work!"), Jimmy had worked for a couple of architectural firms, taking classes along the way. More recently, he had attended a prestigious college at night, paying $50,000 in tuition to get a master's degree in applied urban science and informatics. Now that he had a degree in hand, why was he going back for still more school? As a married man in his late twenties, Jimmy couldn't afford to mess around like this. He needed to get his act together. Or so I thought.

I checked in with Jimmy every so often over the following months as he studied full-time in coding boot camp. He seemed to enjoy it, but I wasn't convinced. Imagine my surprise and delight in the spring of 2021 when Jimmy proudly told me he had landed a great new job as a senior software developer at a well-known technology firm in the retail space. His total compensation: Not $100,000. Not $150,000. No, my seemingly directionless faux nephew would be earning $230,000 in salary and stock options. *Yowsa!*

Jimmy had proved his faux aunt Jill wrong. As he told me, he had found not only a great job but also his calling. "I love working with computers," he said. "I think it's a pretty incredible thing to be able to write some code and then have the computer perform increasingly complex tasks as you build on it."

As Jimmy related, he had made the radical choice of quitting his job because he saw urban planning as a dead end and a fairly thankless career. "I think the pandemic gave us time to consider what our future was going to be," he said, "because it was a lot of time sitting at home on the couch, talking about stuff, and trying to figure out what life would look like after this all ended." For Jimmy, as for so many others, the pandemic accelerated shifts that were already brewing, making a big move more palatable than it otherwise might have been.

But here's the real point of Jimmy's story: the strong connection between education and Great Money Resets. Many people who consider making a major money reset make obtaining more education part of the mix. They might want to improve their job prospects or earnings in their current career. They might wish to cultivate the skills they need to leap headlong into an entirely new career. They might not know what they want and think of going back to school as a perfect way station while they figure it out.

Many times, acquiring more education helps us advance in our professional lives, as it did in Jimmy's case, but quite often it leads us down a costly and time-consuming path. We delve deep into our savings or take out loans, becoming knowledge-rich and cash-poor. Instead of improving our future prospects, we wind up damaging them.

Before you rush to send in that fat tuition payment, and before you potentially even quit your job to go back to school, think critically about whether amassing more education makes sense for you at this point in time. Maybe it does, but maybe not. Even if it does, other, less costly educational options exist that you might not have considered. Please, listen to your concerned aunt Jill on this. To make sure that you really are making a rational choice, here is a simple, three-step analysis you can run through as you plot out your Great Money Reset.

Step #1: Identify the Precise Skills, Knowledge, or Credentials You Hope to Gain by Going Back to School and How Your Career Will Benefit

The boot camp Jimmy attended wasn't for the faint of heart. Intended to mimic actual working conditions, it lasted a year and demanded a crazy number of hours each week—more than your typical job. It wasn't cheap, either. In addition to a nominal monthly fee, Jimmy had to pay 18 percent of his first year's salary to the coding school. But that's just the beginning of what going back to school cost Jimmy. We must also think about opportunity costs and count the $75,000 he would have made had he spent that year working instead of learning to code. Although Jimmy didn't have to take out any education loans, his career transition wound up costing him at least $115,000 all in.

That math worked out well for Jimmy, as he nearly tripled his former salary. But it could have worked out differently if he had struggled to find a job or if he had settled for one that paid less (one offer he received came with a starting salary of only $120,000, for instance). As Jimmy told me, he felt comfortable taking the risk because his wife had a stable, well-paying job, the rent on their apartment was affordable, and they had a supportive family they could count on in case of unanticipated hardship. Jimmy also knew that companies at the time had a seemingly unquenchable thirst for talented computer programmers, making it likely that he'd get a job with little trouble after his boot camp ended.

In his case, paying for boot camp made sense for another important reason: *Jimmy needed new skills in order to reach his career objective.* Having been briefly exposed to computer programming at a previous job thanks to a course he had taken, Jimmy suspected that he might like coding. But while he knew he could get into the field without a college degree (talented kids do that all the time), no company would hire him if he didn't know his JavaScript from his Python. In other words, Jimmy had to actually know how to code in order to get a job. Although I didn't realize it at first, boot camp was an eminently practical choice, a relatively quick way for him to learn everything he needed to join a company and start contributing as a programmer.

Before you decide to retrain, think about precisely which new skills, knowledge, or credentials you must acquire and how your career might benefit. Many people who pursue graduate degrees of one sort or another don't do this. Often, they go back to school because they presume they should, not because they've run a careful analysis and concluded that it's necessary in pursuit of their dreams. Maybe their parents are telling them that they'll never amount to anything if they don't get their law degree. Or maybe they see all of their friends getting an M.B.A. and presume they must, too, in order to move into the senior leadership ranks.

Emotional considerations figure prominently here. Many young people I speak with harbor some notion that they'll feel more confident with more education or that other people will take them more seriously. They might want a degree from a top institution just to feel pride, a sense of accomplishment, or a sense of belonging in an elite club. Maybe they want to pursue a passion of theirs and feel that a higher degree is the best route open to them. These considerations are all understandable. But from a financial standpoint, is it worth spending our or our parents' hard-earned money—potentially hundreds of thousands of dollars—or going deep into debt just to feel proud, accomplished, and less of a fraud, or to pursue a passion?

Sometimes a fancy degree is warranted—not necessarily because of the skills you'll obtain, but because of the credential itself. Cynthia, a friend of mine, dreamed of one day becoming a journalist at a major newspaper. Having grown up in a small town out west, she attended state school for college, obtaining a degree in journalism. Afterward, she applied to every journalism job she could find—many dozens of them—and got absolutely nowhere. She landed at her hometown newspaper, covering town hall meetings and local real estate transactions as she learned the craft of reporting. But after a few years, Cynthia hit a dead end. There was no room for advancement at the paper, and although she had more experience than during her first job search, the result was the same: a pile of rejection letters. The problem, she realized, was that despite her best efforts, she had nothing on her résumé that was setting her apart and allowing her to break in.

One approach to building her résumé was flying out to a war zone somewhere on her own dime and risking her neck getting an earthshaking scoop that would win her a Pulitzer. Another, saner path was to try to get a degree from a top journalism school. Cynthia wound up getting admitted to Columbia, one of the most prestigious journalism programs out there. A master's degree ran Cynthia well into six figures, but it turned out to be magic. As she neared graduation, she began getting interviews—and not just a few. She could finally break into a career she loved.

Even as I tell this story, I feel compelled to counsel caution. Some prestigious degrees might seem like good bets even though they're really not. I know any number of aspiring writers, artists, and actors who spent six figures on M.F.A. degrees from prestigious institutions only to find themselves scratching out a living and saddled with massive amounts of debt.[1] Likewise, if you dream of pursuing a Ph.D. at a top school and finding a plum job in academia, you might want

---

[1] Sophie Haigney, "$78,000 of Debt for a Harvard Theater Degree," *The New York Times*, August 7, 2017, https://www.nytimes.com/2017/08/07/theater/harvard-graduate-theater-debt.html.

to think again. Even before the pandemic, the academic job market was "bleak," as one newspaper report put it.[2] Graduates of top programs had to scrape around for positions at smaller, less glamorous schools. Other Ph.D.s saw themselves competing for scraps—low-paying jobs as adjunct professors, with no benefits. Was it worth the years of effort and financial expenditure to obtain those degrees? The answer for many was not so much.

You might accuse me of being a curmudgeon who is discouraging people from pursuing their passion. "Hey, Jill," you say, "stop spoiling our vibe!" I'm not trying to spoil anyone's vibe. I'm just counseling a teensy-tiny bit of realism. It's great to make a living doing what you love, but is it really your passion to live for years, even decades, under a mound of debt? Is it your passion to find yourself in your fifties with hardly anything saved for retirement and forced to hit up friends and family for help when your kid experiences a medical emergency? Please, pursue your passion, but temper it with a dose of practicality, at least when it comes to investing in education.

Ask yourself: Will my earning potential increase significantly once I have my new degree or certification, and by how much? Will I find it easier to move into a new career or to get a new and better job in my present one? Will I enjoy more job security? Will more education open up new and attrac-

---

2 Kevin Carey, "The Bleak Job Landscape of Adjunctopia for Ph.D.s," *The New York Times*, updated March 6, 2020, https://www.nytimes.com /2020/03/05/upshot/academic-job-crisis-phd.html.

tive opportunities to venture out on my own as a contractor or freelancer? Will it allow me to select from job opportunities in a wider geographic area or to appeal to new kinds of employers (big, established companies, say, as opposed to small, local ones)? The more benefits to education you can pin down and the clearer these benefits are, the more compelling the case for going back to school becomes.

When you think through questions like this, you might well find that going back to school is precisely the *wrong* choice. Let me tell you about Janet, another twentysomething child of a friend of mine. After graduating from college in 2016 with a dual major in economics and science and technology studies, Janet has worked at a series of jobs doing marketing and brand strategy work. The summer after she graduated, she took the GMAT exam, which she would need if she ever decided to go for an M.B.A. degree. She did it somewhat on a whim: She had a few months off before her first job started and didn't have much else to do, so she figured why not? She killed the exam, scoring higher than she expected, making it more likely that she would get in if she ever applied to a prestigious school.

Over the next several years, Janet thought periodically about taking a break from work and getting her M.B.A., but she never went through with it. By early 2021, she was getting itchy in her current job, so the question arose once again: Should she go back to school? Her parents urged her to do it and told her they would happily pay for it. They felt certain that an M.B.A. from a top school would greatly increase her long-term job prospects and land her in a more prestigious company.

Janet wasn't so sure. She was doing well in her career, making about $120,000 a year. The skills and experience she had built up as a consultant were extremely marketable: Nearly every week she'd field a call from a headhunter asking her to consider a new opportunity. Even if her parents would help with the tuition, taking two years away from work came with a huge opportunity cost. And when Janet thought about the specific benefits an M.B.A. might confer, she was underwhelmed. Because she had been working in business and had majored in economics, she felt that she already had a lot of the business knowledge that she would be exposed to in graduate school.

Having a fancy school on her résumé wouldn't hurt, nor would the alumni network she could access upon graduation. On the whole, though, Janet didn't think an M.B.A. would supercharge her career as much as her parents presumed. "I'm willing to believe that an M.B.A. could increase my lifetime earnings," she said. "But I don't think it's a huge difference. The experience I'm getting on the job is making me a better employee. I'm pretty convinced that when it comes to actually acquiring new skills, two years of working versus attending business school will probably be better for me in terms of allowing me to get shit done and grow in my role."

Another consideration loomed large in Janet's thinking when it came to the potential benefits of an M.B.A.: her emotional welfare. Would getting an M.B.A. make her happier in either the short or long term? She didn't think so. "I'm just very happy where I am right now. I like my job—it's going well. I like working in the consulting world. And I like where I'm living." The prospect of shaking up her life didn't appeal, nor did Janet yearn for the experience of being a student again. Every time she heard friends or colleagues talk about business school, she couldn't get excited about it.

When I checked in with Janet in the fall of 2021, she had recently taken a new job rather than apply to M.B.A. programs. Although she continued to favor working rather than going back to school, she admitted that she was still not dead set against making a move. I don't know what the right path for her is, but she might well be right to pass up an M.B.A. degree. As I've seen many times over, these Gen Z kids are often smarter than we boomers or Gen X think. I'm impressed that Janet didn't simply assume that undertaking a Great Money Reset was the right move, and that she didn't simply listen to her parents. She looked hard at the potential benefits—including those related to both her career and her personal happiness—and questioned whether they were really all that. You should do the same.

Step #2: How Would You Pay for It?

I'm lucky I have so many "nieces" and "nephews," and even luckier that their stories are perfect for this chapter. One of my wonderful, twentysomething faux nieces, Jen, was a huge fan of music and the arts. After college, she scored a job working for a small, independent theater company making about $50,000—enough to get by in New York City as a single person in a crowded apartment, but not much more than that. Jen nourished dreams of one day running a big cultural institution—something like Lincoln Center or the Metropolitan Opera. As she looked into it, she realized that although cultural institutions are nonprofits, the administrators running them had to know about business in order not to drive them off a cliff. If she were ever to move into such a role, she'd need a business background, too—something she sorely lacked.

The solution was the very degree that Janet pooh-poohed: an M.B.A. Unfortunately, Jen had few resources of her own to draw on in order to obtain one. She might have either asked her parents to pay a couple of hundred thousand for the degree or taken on piles of debt that she'd be paying back forever. Instead, to her immense credit, she got plucky, searching far and wide for scholarships, grants, and special programs that help underpaid people in the arts afford graduate degrees.

To her delight, she found quite a few opportunities available for people like her who wanted to transfer to a new job role or career. One of the best of these was a program at a prestigious business school that would allow her to earn an M.B.A. *for free*. Even better, the program came with a $10,000 annual stipend to help with living expenses. Jen would still have to do without the $100,000 in earnings she would have made had she continued to work during two years of graduate school, and she'd have to come up with some funds of her own to pay for living expenses. But this program allowed her to get the advanced degree she needed and emerge debt-free.

Jen enrolled and graduated with her M.B.A. Afterward, she transitioned into exactly the kind of job she had envisioned, landing a six-figure salary as the head of strategy with a well-respected cultural organization in the Midwest. Not too shabby!

When considering whether to go back to school, don't just consider the potential benefits. Assess, too, how you're going to pay for it. You might be tempted to think about this decision as a simple cost-benefit analysis, but in truth the cost side of the equation isn't so simple. First, there might be some costs associated with going back to school that you haven't considered. We've talked about opportunity cost if you already hold a job. But you'll also have to figure out a way to afford healthcare and other benefits that your employer is currently covering for you. If you already have outstanding debt for education or a car, will you still have to make the monthly payments?

Once you've pinned down the actual costs, consider what you must sacrifice to come up with the money. Will your parents or some other rich relative foot the bill? Fantastic! But then again, maybe not. As we'll see in Chapter 9, family help usually comes with emotional baggage, even if you don't have to repay the money. Parents who pay the expenses of their grown children tend to feel that they can tell them what to do—not something that many adults want to endure, especially at a time of great change and opportunity.

If you're going to come up with the funds yourself, you might face some difficult choices. Let's say you're thirty-eight years old and earning $150,000, and you want to attend graduate school. You might be able to afford that, but it might mean you must wait longer before you can buy a house. Or perhaps you'll be saving less for retirement each year for the foreseeable future. Or forgoing private school for your kids. Given your analysis of the career benefits graduate school might yield, getting a graduate degree might still wind up being the best long-term move for you and your family. But you'll have to think through the numbers and the larger ramifications to come up with the right answer.

When reviewing options for financing education, one to avoid is pulling money from your retirement accounts or borrowing against those assets. If you're thirty-eight, you make $150,000 each year working at a good job, and you have $300,000 in your 401(k), you might think it's fine to borrow $100,000. It's not fine. It's a massive risk. What if a year or two from now you lose your job and can't repay the loan? At that point, the government considers the loan a withdrawal and hits you with a 10 percent penalty for withdrawing early. Also, you'll have to pay taxes on that $100,000 as if it were ordinary income.

In 2022, your $150,000 in income would put you in the 24 percent federal tax bracket (we're assuming that you're single). The loan that you took would now be a distribution, which would cost you $10,000 in early withdrawal penalties (levied on money taken out before age fifty-nine and a half) and $24,000 in added tax liabilities, for a total of $34,000.

All of a sudden, you would have only $166,000 in your re-
tirement account instead of $300,000. That's a pretty dev-
astating hit to your future. If you're thinking of borrowing
against your retirement savings, I'd much rather see you
take out an education loan, either from the government or
from a private lender. Take those no-good, grubby hands
out of your retirement pot!

Another question I often get is whether someone in their
late thirties or forties should refinance their mortgage to fund
graduate school. The answer is . . . it depends (I know, helpful). How much equity do you have in your home? Are you
even able to take more out? And if you do, how much would
the higher mortgage amount add to your monthly payment?
Could you make those payments without killing yourself at a
second job or sacrificing your lifestyle in ways you can't bear?

For any educational loan you might consider taking, how
long would you require to pay it back? Would you be saddled for decades with debt you can't seem to shake? Could
you handle the psychological impact of that? Again, would
you have to forgo other goals, like paying for your kids' college or owning your own home? And would those sacrifices
be worth it given the financial or career benefits you hope to
gain from more education? If you think they might be, how
certain are those financial benefits, really? Do you know for a
fact that your employer or another will put you into a higher-
paying job once you have a degree in hand, or is that possibility more theoretical? These are all questions you must
carefully consider before taking on more debt.

Step #3: Are There Any Cheaper Ways to Get Where You Want to Go?

Did I mention I have lots of faux nieces and nephews? Another of them, Jeff, started his career during the 2000s as a sportswriter working for a local semiprofessional league. He thought he would be the next Frank Deford, but after a few years, he found that the whole sports scene was getting old—he just didn't like the work that much. Further, with the rise of online media, career prospects for journalists didn't seem so bright. The digital world was where it was at. But how could he break in and get a job working at a dot-com property? He had no background in it and knew little about technology.

One option might have been to go back to school and get a master's degree or some other credential that would expose him to digital technology. But Jeff had a better idea. His company was developing a sports-related online media business of its own. Maybe he could leverage his existing skills, interest in sports, and knowledge of the company to work for this business. That's exactly what Jeff did. After getting a new role, he spent a number of months learning about the dot-com world and then took on responsibility for product development and sales. In his new job, he was now perfectly positioned for a more remunerative career in digital media and commerce, without having to spend a dime reskilling himself.

After you've pondered what more education might give you, what it could cost, and how you might fund it, analyze whether any cheaper alternatives exist. As Jeff's story suggests, you might try to gain new skills or knowledge informally by volunteering for specific job roles or projects that provide strong learning opportunities. This route isn't without cost: You might have to agree to work for less than you currently make, relocate geographically, give up status or power inside your organization, or make other compromises. But you can avoid hefty bills for graduate school as well as the opportunity cost of taking a year or two or more away from full-time work.

If you do need to obtain a formal educational credential, cheaper alternatives might still exist. Would your employer pay for reskilling via a corporate training program or a tuition reimbursement benefit? Must you really get a four-year degree, or would a two-year degree or even a nontraditional program do the trick, like coding boot camp did for my nephew Jimmy? Must you attend a prestigious but pricey university, or would a cheaper state school option also work?

You might presume that obtaining your degree from a prestigious institution is your best move, but that's not necessarily true. In many cases, employers don't care where you obtained a credential so long as you have it. Another so-called niece ("Jill, enough with the faux nieces and nephews already!") worked as a teacher in the New York City schools. She knew she would qualify for an automatic salary increase if she had a master's degree in education. She got into a fancy-pants, name-brand program, which would cost her well into six figures and require her to attend full-time. She also gained admission to a program from a less prestigious institution that she could pursue part-time while continuing to work and that would only cost a few thousand dollars a year. Some in her family urged her to go to fancy-pants U, enamored as they were by the prestige of that august institution. But she realized she would learn what she needed from the cheaper program, and she wouldn't earn any less with a degree from there.

Setting aside any little overachiever voices bouncing around her head, she chose the cheaper option. She graduated, got the pay bump she wanted, and is now living happily ever after—with more financial security than she might have had if she'd had to pay big bucks and take time off work.

If someone else is footing your education bill for you, you might well choose to pursue the fancier degree. But if you're bankrolling it, it behooves you to be more pragmatic. Yes, you could choose the most expensive possible educational option, but you're rolling the dice with your financial future. Stop thinking about how cool your résumé would look with an Ivy League school on it or with a Ph.D. instead of just a master's. Focus on how to get the skills you need as cheaply and efficiently as possible. Strike a healthy balance between your educational aspirations and your other financial goals.

A Lesson from the Coach

A friend of mine, Andy, harbored relatively simple career dreams. A talented basketball player in high school, he wanted to become an English teacher and coach high school ball.

Alas, life had other plans for him. Andy's family was quite wealthy, and he felt pressure to go to law school and then join the family's real estate business as a general counsel. Andy acquiesced, becoming a lawyer and joining the company. For a while, it worked well enough for him. Although he didn't particularly like what he did, he made a lot of money and was able to fund a nice lifestyle for himself and his growing family.

By the time Andy reached his forties, this compromise began to break down. He found himself increasingly miserable at work and yearning for more passion and excitement in life. He seriously considered quitting his job, going back to school, and fulfilling his earlier dream of working as a teacher. He knew that the costs of doing so would be astronomical in terms of lost income, but he wasn't sure what else to do. He couldn't continue indefinitely hating what he did during his seemingly endless workweek.

For a while, Andy muddled on. But then an idea occurred to him. He approached a local high school basketball coach and asked if he needed any help with his team. He told the coach that he hadn't been good enough to play in college but that he loved the game and was an avid student of it. He thought he could help kids on the team develop as players and as people. The coach agreed and made Andy assistant coach on a volunteer basis. Andy continued to work as general counsel, but since he enjoyed seniority at his job, he could adjust his schedule as he liked, making time to attend afternoon practices and games. He served as an assistant coach for a number of years and absolutely loved it. He no longer was so miserable, since he had a meaningful outlet for his passion. When the coach retired, Andy took on his position.

Reskilling is indeed a critically important part of your Great Money Reset. It can help you shift to a new career or advance in your current one, and you can also use it as an opportunity to take a pause and figure out what to do with your life. But formal education isn't the be-all and end-all, and it almost certainly isn't worth sacrificing your financial future over. Be prudent about your educational choices and closely map out the costs and benefits before taking any action. Think creatively about your options. Don't necessarily go for the fancy graduate degree. And at the extreme, you might not need to go back to school at all or make any change in your professional career, as Coach Andy found out.

Think critically about how education will benefit you, what it will cost, and how else you might reach your goals. Don't pursue change and growth at all costs. Aim for change and growth that make sense *for you*.

Rock the Reset

- Before you rush to go back to school as part of a Great Money Reset, think critically about whether more education really makes sense for you.

- Perform a three-part analysis, identifying what you hope to gain from more schooling, how you might pay for it, and whether any less costly options exist for reaching your career goals.

- Think creatively. Don't necessarily go for the big, fancy graduate degree. You might not need to go back to school at all or make any change in your professional career.

9

Family Planning (No, Not That Kind)

Family relationships matter when you're making a Great Money Reset. This chapter helps you navigate those relationships so that they're as harmonious and supportive as possible.

Rebecca, a friend of mine living in the Detroit area, always prided herself on putting her family first. When her three kids were small, she gave up her career to become a stay-at-home mom. As a professional, she only knew how to do a job one way: the right way. She threw herself into the role of chief operating officer of the household, doing the shopping and cleaning, volunteering for PTA assignments, hosting sleepovers, and stoically trucking her kids between soccer matches. She prided herself on being there for every bruised knee or boyfriend disaster, leaving it to her husband,

Gene, to support the family. He did a good job of it, too, earning about $650,000 per year as a successful marketing executive.

One day in early 2020, when the two of them were in their early fifties, Gene came home with some exciting news. A fast-growing start-up out in Los Angeles had offered him a job, and he wanted to take it. He was burned out after years with his current employer, and trading dreary Detroit winters for the SoCal lifestyle sounded appealing. He and Rebecca had always dreamed about living in a warmer climate—now was their chance to actually do it. The new job only paid around $300,000, but with no kids to worry about (they were all in their late twenties or early thirties by this time, fully launched in their careers), he and Rebecca would get by just fine. Life was short. Why the heck *not* do something a little crazy?

Rebecca was game, so the couple took a closer look at their finances to confirm they could do it. The new job was a bit of a risk: Gene couldn't say whether the start-up would be around in five to seven years, when he planned to retire. On the flip side, if it did succeed, he'd likely get a nice payday. Running the numbers, the couple established that they could in fact take this risk without dramatically impacting their future retirement plans or their current living standards. But there was one caveat. In recent years, the couple periodically had provided financial support to their kids, paying for graduate school, trips, and incidental expenses as they arose. If they went through with this major money reset, that support would have to end for at least the next five to seven years until the couple began tapping their retirement savings.

Rebecca and Gene decided to go for it and to go big. They wouldn't just move to California—they would make a clean break, selling their big family home in Michigan. They didn't want to think about plodding through another harsh winter. And Rebecca decided that she wanted to embark on an entirely new adventure without any other responsibilities weighing her down. She wanted to focus exclusively on her marriage for a change and on enjoying life. She'd spent so long taking care of her kids. Now it was time for *her* to feel fulfilled.

You might think that their three children, upon hearing of this decision, would support this Great Money Reset after all their parents had done for them. Think again. The kids were hugely disappointed, and they let their parents know it. How *dare* Rebecca and Gene sell the family home? Where would they stay if they wanted to go to their hometown and visit their childhood friends? How could their parents decide not to help them out any longer? Didn't their parents know that they would be buying their first homes soon and would need assistance with their down payments?

These comments might sound pretty tone-deaf for so-called adults, but they are more common than you think. Conflicts crop up when people attempt Great Money Resets—with kids, parents, spouses, close friends—and they can be quite dispiriting. Given how hard it can be to make a big change in our living situation or career, we want to feel like we can depend on our family members for emotional and financial support. We feel empowered when we receive positive responses; utterly bereft, frustrated, and pissed off when we don't.

To succeed with our plans, we must learn to handle close family relationships so that we gain the most wisdom and support possible, no matter what course of action we choose. We must find a path forward that allows us to maintain strong, loving bonds with our relatives, even when they fail to understand our need to change or disagree with our decisions. It comes down to communicating clearly, listening to well-intended advice, establishing boundaries, and sticking by our decisions. As I've found, three key relationship issues arise when we undertake a Great Money Reset, and it's important to get them right. Let's look at each in turn.

Relationship Issue #1: Should I Listen to My Family Members' Advice?

Years ago, when I was thinking of shifting from working as a financial planner to becoming an on-air financial expert, I found myself in a situation that was simultaneously wonderful and difficult. It looked like CBS was going to offer me a job and that I'd be able to move back to my hometown, New York City—that's the wonderful part. At the same time, I had to leave the lucrative financial planning profession where I had spent fourteen years paying my dues and working around the clock to prove myself. Washing my hands of that business would mean I would have to forgo substantial future income that would have landed me on Easy Street. This sum wasn't life-changing, but at the time, it felt like I would be abandoning what was close to a sure thing.

I was really torn up about the idea of forgoing this money. What if I came to regret it? I wanted to undertake my Great Money Reset, but I didn't know that I could. Well, that's not true: My gut told me to let the money go and move on with my life, but I was taking a big risk and needed (or wanted) someone close to me to tell me I wasn't crazy.

I considered approaching my mother but quickly thought better of it. My mom is very supportive of me, but when it comes to money matters, she tends to be extremely conservative. She's not entrepreneurial and focuses pretty exclusively on one priority: financial security. Given her bias, I knew what she would say: *Don't even think about leaving that money behind.* I'm all for financial security, but I also knew that I had to make a decision that would take into account my own happiness. The reality was I didn't like working as a financial planner and money manager anymore, and I really wanted to move back to New York City to try something new. Those feelings mattered, too.

My father, on the other hand, seemed like he'd be able to give me advice based on a more balanced view. After spending his career working on Wall Street, he understood money. But for reasons that I'll explain later, he also knew there was much more to life than money.

When I approached him, I wasn't disappointed. In fact, his advice has stayed with me ever since. "Honey," he said, "in your mind, you've already made your decision. I know you don't want to leave behind the money. And I know it feels like a lot of money. But I'll tell you right now, that money won't be meaningful to you if it drags you back down to a dark place and prevents you from moving on fully to the next career you've envisioned."

Wow. My father nailed it. He was able to understand the conflicting emotions I was having, acknowledge that I'd already made a choice in my own mind, and provide me with a powerful rationale for going through with that choice. He didn't try to argue against what I'd already decided or change my mind. He listened intently and offered advice that would allow me to proceed more decisively, calmly, and confidently down the path I'd chosen.

Should you listen to what your family members say? The answer is a mushy "it depends." If a family member offers you unsolicited advice, you'll obviously want to consider what unconscious biases might be coloring their perspective, as well as what their conscious motivations might be. Do they really want what's best for you? Even if they think they do, do they still have a personal stake in convincing you to make a specific choice? Are their values, interests, or temperament at odds with yours? More broadly, do you respect their judgment, both in general and about the specific topics at hand? Have they offered advice in the past that is wise, balanced, reasonable, and insightful?

If you don't think about these kinds of considerations, you

might wind up paying too much heed to feedback that isn't helpful. Many successful people can share stories of naysayers who told them early in their careers that they would fail. A cable news executive who was happy to have me appear as an unpaid guest on the upstart cable network in 2007–2008 told me I'd never make it in radio as a full-timer because the timbre of my voice was all screwed up. (Schadenfreude alert: He was fired and never found another job, while I have a pretty decent career doing TV, radio, podcasting, and voice-over work.) A writer friend of mine had a graduate school professor tell him he lacked enough imagination to ever make it as a writer; he's made millions tapping at the keyboard. Sometimes such judgments are correct and worth listening to, but many times they simply reflect biases, lack of judgment, or bad intentions on the part of the person giving advice. Save yourself some angst and weed out people who aren't giving you or won't give you balanced, insightful advice.

In addition to deciding if you should listen to unsolicited advice from close relatives, you should also consider whether to approach them proactively and *ask* for advice. Good counsel is important, but try to go into these conversations knowing precisely what you're looking to achieve. If you find yourself attempting to obtain permission from a parent or other family member, you might want to reflect on that. As an adult, do you still want to put yourself in the position of asking permission? There might be some issues related to your own self-esteem and sense of agency that require some attention. I know that these feel like soft issues to consider when it comes to money, but in my experience, unless you deal with them, the reset you so desire could be at risk.

A better reason to request guidance about a Great Money Reset is to support your own introspection. Many people find themselves in the situation I was in. They've thought through the decision backward and forward. They've run the numbers with every conceivable variable. They think they know what they want to do, but the downsides are giving them pause. Are they *really* comfortable taking a risk and opening themselves up to some potentially significant consequences?

Family members can help not just because of any particular wisdom they possess, but because they know us better than most. When I first got to CBS, one of the hair and makeup people gave me very good advice. She said, "When you're on the air, the people who know you best will tell you when you look and perform at your best. It's often best to trust in that." As this woman explained, everyone around me would have some kind of opinion (and believe me, they still do!), but my close relatives would be able to see the nuances and tell me when I appeared most comfortable and self-assured. They also would be *willing* to tell me if something looked wrong.

This woman was on to something, and her insight applies to money just as well as to hair and makeup. When we're struggling to decide on a path forward, relatives can remind us of parts of ourselves we might be forgetting in the moment. They can alert us to our own biases, which they probably know all too well. They can sense if we're in thrall to our emotions and can alert us to this. They might understand patterns of dysfunction that exist in our family and can offer perspective on whether our decisions are perpetuating those patterns without us even realizing it. And they might be more willing than others around us to tell us the truth, including the parts we don't wish to hear.

To obtain the best possible advice from your relatives, be clear both with yourself and with them at the outset about what you do and don't want from them. Are you still in the "what if" stage and want someone to brainstorm possibilities with you? Are you honestly torn about a decision and unable to decide? Do you need someone to walk through the pros and cons with you and perhaps give you the benefit of their knowledge and experience? Or have you already more or less come to a decision and simply want to make sure that you haven't missed anything and that you've thought through the main issues in a logical fashion?

It's interesting: Sometimes we ask for advice from a relative precisely so that we can feel good about doing the *opposite* of what they suggest. A friend of mine, Carl, attended a prestigious law school on a scholarship when he was in his late twenties but found after a single semester that he absolutely hated it. He excelled in his tough first-year classes and made some good friends, but he felt so anxious that he didn't get a single good night's sleep throughout the entire semester. By the end of the semester, simply walking into the lecture hall was giving him a panic attack.

Pondering his feelings during Christmas break, Carl

realized he'd made a dreadful mistake. His father was a very successful lawyer, and if Carl was being honest with himself, he had applied to law school because he hadn't known what else to do. He had thought a law degree would at least give him a way to earn a decent living. Rather than forcing himself to grind out a living doing something he didn't really like, Carl realized that he needed to drop out of law school and spend some time figuring himself out. He didn't know what he would do next, but he had to have faith that he'd figure it out instead of blindly following his father's path.

When Carl officially informed an administrator at the law school that he was dropping out, the administrator was dumbstruck. Was he really turning down a scholarship at a prestigious law school? Indeed he was. Just before making this call, Carl spoke with his father to tell him of his choice and gauge his reaction. On some level, Carl was hoping that his father would empathize with him and confirm that he was making the right choice for *him*, even if it was not what his father would have done.

Instead, Carl's father urged him to reconsider and told him that he was making the biggest mistake of his life. Something about his father's tone led Carl to an epiphany. He'd been listening to his father all his life, and it was no longer working for him. He needed to strike out on his own. It was good, in a sense, that his father was so adamant about his position. Carl realized he would have to be equally adamant about his own. And in truth, he *did* know that law school was wrong for him. After that phone call with his father, he felt more emboldened than ever—if still a bit nervous—to finally strike out on his own. He wound up making a decision that in retrospect proved pivotal in his life, leading to a rich and meaningful career, among other things.

We should listen to advice from our family members. But we should do it thoughtfully, and we shouldn't always agree with them or do exactly what they say. Let's remember at all times that *we're* the ones making the decision. We should ask our relatives for advice in order to fuel our own introspection and decision-making process, not replace it. And when it comes time to make a call, let's reserve agency for the one person who must bear the greatest consequences of all: us.

Relationship Issue #2: Should I Accept Financial Help from a Family Member?

Many people grow wiser with age. They leave behind the stupid conflicts and disputes that used to bother them when they were younger. A woman I know, Samantha, is not one of these people. She's eighty-five years old and hasn't spoken to her younger brother for decades. Why? Well, all those years ago when Samantha's parents died, Samantha felt she didn't get as much of an inheritance as she should have. Her brother, Barry, had borrowed money from their parents to buy his first home, and he had never paid it back. By all rights, half of that money belonged to her (they were the only two siblings and each inherited half of their parents' estate).

Barry disputed Samantha's account, claiming that he had in fact paid their parents back. She claimed that her mother had told her before she died that he hadn't and that her mother was intending to resolve it with him. The two stopped talking over the issue, even though the amount of money in question wasn't meaningful to either of them, given their financial positions.

Before you criticize Samantha as petty, let's acknowledge that financial disputes among family members often reflect deep, unresolved relationship issues. Money is simply one way that these become tangible. Let's also note that these kinds of disputes are extraordinarily common. And that's because many people make a big mistake when they take money from a family member or offer to provide a relative with financial support. They don't document the transaction and the expectations that surround it.

If you're thinking of asking a relative for financial help, for heaven's sake, determine if it's going to be a loan or a gift, and if it's a loan, detail the terms of that loan. Then write it all down. And record it when the loan has been repaid. If you don't, all kinds of misunderstandings can occur. You might think the money is a gift when it really isn't. You might presume you have latitude about if or when to pay back a loan, when in fact your relative expects some sort of regular payments. Your relative might give you a loan with laid-back terms but expect you to help *them* in a time of financial need. You might pay back your relative only to find that they don't remember you having done so.

If you go into these kinds of conversations with the intention of documenting the transactions, you will often wind up with important clarity about expectations. During the pandemic, a friend of mine who was going through a rough time asked to borrow $10,000 from me. I knew that she had experienced considerable adversity in her life and would have a hard time ever paying me back, so I gave her the money as a gift, specifying that I had zero expectation she'd ever pay it back. She declined, saying that she didn't feel comfortable accepting a gift. I countered that I didn't feel comfortable loaning her the money, so if she didn't agree to take it as a gift, I wouldn't give it to her.

In the end, I gave her the money—as a gift, not a loan. This distinction was important to me. I had the money and was happy to help her. If I were giving the money as a loan, I would expect to be repaid, and she would know that I harbored that expectation. Any failure on her part to repay it would cause unnecessary tension and weirdness in our relationship. It might not for another person, but I knew it would for me.

Whatever your attitudes about giving money to others, it's important to be as clear as possible about what you expect, both in your own mind and in your conversations with others. And if you're asking for money, be methodical about it. Explain what you're doing and why you need the money. Explain how much money you'll need and what kind of transaction you envision. If it's a loan, propose a plan for how you'll pay it back. And propose an arrangement for a backup plan in case you can't repay the money as you planned. In Samantha's case, her brother might have stipulated at the outset with his elderly parents that if he didn't pay them back on time, they should state in their will that he should receive that much less as an inheritance.

As you can gather from this discussion, I do think we can ask for or accept financial help from our relatives to fund our Great Money Resets. That said, I wouldn't rush to do it. Whether we realize it or not, gifts or loans of money among family members always come with expectations that can poison otherwise healthy relationships or totally blow up already tenuous ones. In many families, gifts of money from a parent to an adult child come with unspoken expectations that the parent can have a say in the child's decisions. If you're the child, do you really want to give your parents that kind of authority over you? Do you want to spend your time and energy pushing back when your parent tries to tell you what to do? This is to say nothing of your siblings, who might resent that your parent is helping you out and therefore has less for them. Wouldn't it be easier for everyone if you got the money from somewhere else?

Asking a family member for financial help is risky. If you must do it, at least approach it as you would any other business transaction and formalize the transaction. That way, you can protect your family relationships *and* get the financial support you need.

Relationship Issue #3: What Do I Do if My Family Doesn't Support Me?

Just because you ask for help during a Great Money Reset, whether it's financial or emotional, doesn't mean you'll get it. What do you do then?

Let's pick up the story of Rebecca and Gene. When their kids reacted poorly to their decision to sell the family home and relocate out west, I advised the couple to sit down with their kids and explain the decision to them in more detail as well as the bigger picture of their financial life. Although the family was close, Rebecca and Gene had never talked openly and honestly with their kids about money. The kids knew that their dad did well at his job, but they didn't know specifics about the resources the family had at its disposal, nor did they know about Rebecca and Gene's retirement planning.

I also advised Rebecca and Gene to slow down a little. I didn't by any means want them to forgo their dream of moving out west, but was it necessary for them to sell their Michigan home and buy a new one in California right away? Forget about their kids for a moment: It made sense for Rebecca and Gene to hold on to their existing home and rent for a year. That way, they could learn about the local real estate scene and what neighborhoods or living arrangements would best fill their needs. They'd have an off-ramp if it turned out that they had made a mistake and absolutely hated Southern California. Waiting a year to make the transition complete also would give their kids an opportunity to visit them in Southern California and become more comfortable with the situation.

Rebecca and Gene took my advice, and it all worked out. They ran through the numbers with their kids and explained why it meant so much to them to move to California. In particular, they noted that this was the last opportunity that Gene would likely get to make a big move in his career, and it came at a time when he and Rebecca were both young enough to undertake an adventure. Rebecca and Gene also showed their kids that over the long term they probably would still be able to help them financially. As they discovered, their kids' real concern hadn't been about a lack of financial support but rather a fear that their parents wouldn't be there for them emotionally if they were living on the other side of the country (the kids were all living in the Midwest or on the East Coast). Rebecca and Gene assured them that they would be— nothing would change.

Rebecca and Gene found a nice rental in California, and the kids visited them in 2020, quarantining with them for several months during the pandemic. They enjoyed Southern California and acknowledged that the move had been right for their parents. They affirmed that their parents really did deserve to prioritize themselves at this point in their lives, and they agreed that they wanted to see their parents happy during this last phase of their father's career. Gene's new job has been a wild ride, but it's been secure enough that he and Rebecca felt comfortable selling their Michigan home and buying a condo in California. To say that the couple is thrilled with their Great Money Reset is an understatement. Rebecca recently told me that the move had breathed new life into their relationship and allowed her to start a new job from home in marketing. "The decision was scary to make," she said, "but it has proven to be one of the best things we have ever done."

Rebecca and Gene's story holds a couple of lessons for us. First, *don't let your family members guilt you*. Initially, Gene felt awful when faced with his kids' reaction and was tempted to give up their plans for a Great Money Reset. Rebecca, meanwhile, was disappointed at how ungrateful and entitled her kids seemed, and she was determined to enjoy a new life out in California. "I've spent my life giving to these kids," she told me. "Now it's my turn." These diverging feelings created a rift in Rebecca and Gene's relationship, but eventually Gene came around to Rebecca's point of view, and the two proceeded with their plan.

As painful as family conflict can be, we can't simply break when our loved ones push back against our plans for a money reset. When they just don't get it, we have to be strong enough to move ahead anyway and hope they'll eventually come around. Of course, it's important to listen to and acknowledge their concerns to the extent we can, but we must also honor the needs and desires that prompted us to contemplate a big change in the first place. As honorable as sacrificing our own happiness for that of our kids, parents, or other relatives might seem, this likely won't work as a long-term solution. Forcing ourselves to stick with a job, career, home, or relationship that isn't working for us can compromise our mental or physical health. And forgoing our dreams also can wind up weakening our familial bonds, embittering us and causing us to feel resentful toward our loved ones.

When our families harbor serious concerns, we should try to find a solution that allows us to accommodate everyone's needs to a satisfactory extent. Consider my friend David's situation. By the time he reached his mid-forties, David found that he despised his career as a cardiologist. Although he was making great money (about $600,000 to $700,000 a year), he didn't like interacting with patients—he just didn't feel he was any good at it. He did like the parts of his job having to do with medical research, such as reading the latest studies, analyzing them, and figuring out their implications for his practice. He decided that he would try a new career working in the pharmaceutical industry. He was able to land a job fairly quickly, but at a salary of about $200,000, a fraction of what he formerly earned.

When David told his wife Pamela, a plastic surgeon, that he was quitting medicine, she didn't take it well. "You've spent the past eighteen years of your life getting to where you are," she told him. "We've got kids to support. Are you serious?" After her first reaction passed, she and David came up with a plan. She would agree to support him in his new career and hope that he would succeed and that his earnings would take off. In the meantime, the family could make do by relying more on her salary. David would agree to check in with her quarterly and evaluate how they were doing as a family. If the family needed money or other problems arose, David would consider going back to cardiology.

This plan worked. David loved his new job in pharma, and perhaps because he was so happy, he managed to move up the ladder and earn more money. Meanwhile, Pamela leaned in on her career, leaving a hospital job and starting her own practice, which was much more lucrative. Within a few years, the family was doing as well or better financially as it had been, and David was happy.

Kudos to Pamela for working with her husband to help him realize his dream. And kudos to David as well. He didn't fold under pressure when Pamela freaked out, and he didn't take a hard line, either. Working together, the two discovered how David might make the Great Money Reset that he needed to make, but in a way that also acknowledged Pamela's own concerns and accounted for them to the extent possible.

Whenever tension arises or the potential for it exists, communication becomes critical. Take the time to explain your money reset and the consideration that led to it. Delve into the numbers and reveal your thinking. Even if you're the parent of school-age children, you'll want to include them in a frank but calm and age-appropriate conversation about the changes you're contemplating and their financial implications. If your money reset will require sacrifices on the family's part, explain what will have to change as well as what the family will still be able to afford. These are sometimes painful conversations, but they are also necessary ones. Kids usually do better when their parents respect them enough to tell them the truth in a loving and compassionate way.

Remember Alan and Marie from Chapter 6, the couple who, despite earning $320,000 a year, had racked up $110,000 in credit card debt? They couldn't afford to continue living in their current apartment while also paying for private school and summer camp for their three kids. Although they really didn't want to pull their kids out of private school, they did agree to sell their apartment and minimize funding for their kids' college. To get their kids on board, they needed to sit down with them and explain that these decisions were necessary. They could tell their kids that, as a consolation prize, they'd at least be able to stay in their school, which was very important to them. By taking the time to explain the situation to the kids as transparently as possible and to hear the kids' concerns, Alan and Marie could frame their financial difficulties as a problem that the family could tackle together. They'd make it work and get through to the other side.

It's important to come prepared to these conversations. In fact, you can often preempt conflict with close family members by thinking through in advance how you might communicate your decision. Remember Melissa from the Introduction? She received pushback from her parents when she first told them of her decision to quit her well-paying job and spend time traveling the country. But it would have been much worse if she hadn't prepared for the conversation. She had already created a financial plan for herself, and was able to demonstrate to her parents that she wouldn't starve or default on her mortgage if she took some time off. She could also point out to them that she'd already tried to take a month off to see if she would feel happier upon returning to work. Although her parents still disliked her decision, they at least felt better after seeing how responsible and reasonable her thought process was.

When Crackpot Ideas Work Out

I like chapters that end with happy stories, so here's one for you. My friend Keith and his wife, Marcy, were both lawyers. Marcy was killing it in her career, having made partner at a white-shoe law firm. I don't even want to know how much she was making. Keith wasn't so enamored with law, so with Marcy's blessing he quit his job, became a stay-at-home dad to the couple's kids, and spent part of his time trying to make it as a writer. Before long, he achieved some success, landing a publishing deal and receiving accolades for his first book.

About five years ago, Keith phoned me up and told me about an exciting new business venture of his. He was going to invest money in a new independent bookstore that was opening up in his neighborhood. I almost fell out of my chair. *What? Are you kidding me?* Ever since the advent of Amazon, bookstores around the country have been closing. While Keith was at it, maybe he wanted to start a local newspaper. Or perhaps a video store. I couldn't imagine he could make any money, and I thought there was a good chance that he'd lose his entire investment. I told him he was absolutely nuts and should find something else.

Do you think Keith listened to his well-meaning aunt Jill? Not at all. Keith had an intuition that this venture would succeed, and he wanted to listen to that. He knew his investment was risky, but that was okay. The couple had saved a boatload of money and were financially secure, so even if they lost the entire investment, it would not change their lives. Keith wanted to become active in his local literary scene, and this was an interesting way to do it.

A year later, Keith's bookstore opened. It quickly became one of the few independent bookstores in the country that isn't just surviving, but truly kicking ass. Today, Keith is making money and enjoying the literary lifestyle. I'm even talking to him about how to open a second location, while wiping all the egg off my face.

I tell you about Keith to reinforce the point I made earlier: Don't give up on your dream just because a family member (or in this instance, a close friend with a financial background) doesn't get it. Ultimately, you're the best arbiter of what's right for you. I also have a message for all of us would-be advice-givers out there: Let's not rush to judgment so quickly. Just because an idea might look dumb on the surface doesn't mean it's doomed to failure. You really do never know.

Instead of telling our loved ones that they're crazy, try to understand what's driving them to make their decision and whether other, less radical changes might satisfy them. If not, be as supportive as you can, looking for ways to help them minimize their downside risk. You might be right and their plan will fail, but sometimes in life people have to experience failures just to say that they've tried. Sometimes, too, these failures prove to be just what people need to put themselves on the right path. By withholding judgment and trying to be as supportive as possible, we can keep our relationships strong and perhaps be there to lend a helping hand if our loved one ever needs it.

If you're embarking on a Great Money Reset, I hope this chapter has convinced you to make a little family planning (not *that* kind of family planning) part of the mix. Taking the leap toward our dreams can be extremely scary and disorienting. We need all the help we can get, particularly from our close relatives, the people who know and care about us the most. It behooves us to take a little care in managing these relationships. Bear in mind, the changes we make can be difficult for them, too, so how about we *all* show a bit of compassion and understanding for one another during this period of flux?

Putting some thought into how we manage our family relationships is the least we can do, and as I've seen again and again, it can make all the difference.

Rock the Reset

- A Great Money Reset can be tricky when it comes to our close family relationships. We should strive to maintain strong bonds with our relatives, even when they disagree with our decisions.

- Consider three key relationship questions: Should I listen to my family member's advice? Should I take financial help from a family member? What should I do if I don't receive the family support I expected?

- Don't give up on your dream just because a family member doesn't get it. You know best what's right for you.

10

The Virtues
of Going Long

Whether or not you're currently undertaking a major life or career change, it's important to think about your longer-term future and take steps to build financial resilience. Years from now when you want to undertake a Great Money Reset, you'll have a head start.

Agreat many circumstances can spawn a Great Money Reset. It could be a global pandemic, as I've suggested, but it could also be the death of a spouse, a business reversal, a divorce, or the departure of kids for college. In my late father's case, it was a major health scare. In 1992, when Dad was fifty-two years old, he learned that one of his aortic valves was malfunctioning. He had transplant surgery, which was successful, but he started feeling unwell after his discharge from the hospital. On his doctor's advice, he went to the emergency room, and good thing that he did: Doctors found that Dad was experiencing a complication of the surgery—his lungs were filling with fluid. If he'd waited much longer, he would have suffocated.

Shaken by this near-death experience, Dad resolved to make some changes in his life. As he saw it, his need for heart valve surgery meant that he was living on borrowed time. Doctors told him that the valve would probably last another twenty years, but he didn't know if he even had that long. After decades working on the floor of the American Stock Exchange, he'd formed an investment company with a partner and traded their own capital. Although he made decent money, the work was stressful and not enjoyable. Dad couldn't see wasting his precious time on it any longer.

Dad could have quit right then, but it would have meant a significant lifestyle change for my parents. Although they didn't live lavishly, their savings would have to last my mother (and hopefully, Dad, too) decades into the future. After running the numbers with me, he opted for a more gradual approach that would allow him to save a bit more and put his affairs in order. He informed his business partner that over the next four to five years he would phase out his involvement in the firm. He would take a reduced salary during this time, but afterward the partner could take all of the firm's capital and invest it on his own (this was a generous move on my dad's part, I might add, since he had contributed half of the start-up funds). Once Dad left the business, he planned to earn a bit of money each year trading in his spare time. Between that and an investment my mom had, they'd do just fine.

Dad went through with his plan, retiring in his late fifties. He enjoyed a slower, more rewarding pace for about twenty years before dying at the age of seventy-six (of an infection, not a faulty valve). Although he contended with a number of health issues during his last decade, he felt content in general because he was living life on *his* terms. He spent time with his family, played golf, hung out with his friends, and was always up to hear or tell a good story. Because he had planned years in advance for his Great Money Reset, he could move smoothly into his next act at the appropriate time, with the least possible financial or personal disruption.

Many people start thinking about a money reset only *after* a momentous event has shaken up their life. They scramble to reorient their finances, a process that can feel stressful and even impossible. At the very least, undertaking a Great Money Reset on the fly often means that their heightened emotions exercise too much sway over their judgment, and that their options are somewhat narrower than they might have been. They might have benefitted by saving more to prepare for a change, or selling a piece of real estate, or converting more of their Roth retirement savings. Now it's too late.

Life is inherently unpredictable, but we can still antic-ipate many of the money resets we might one day wish to make. If we're in our early fifties, we might anticipate want-ing to retire early or move to a new city before our sixtieth birthday. If we're in our mid-forties, maybe we anticipate downshifting our careers or taking them in a new direction in our early fifties, when our kids leave for college. If we're in our early thirties, we might imagine wanting to start a new business, moving to a different part of the country, or going back to school in five or six years once we've gotten married and settled down. If we're married in our mid- or late twenties, we might anticipate having ourselves or our partner work less and stay home to take care of our as-yet-unborn kids.

Whatever the specific scenario, planning in advance for a potential Great Money Reset can benefit us enormously. By allowing us to maximize the financial resources at our disposal, it can make the difference between having to work a part-time job to get by or having more leisure time, or between being able to have a luxurious retirement home or one that is more modestly appointed. Less tangibly, advance planning can allow us to break through our fears and actually take a big step, as it gives us time to acclimate ourselves emotionally to the idea of change. Thinking proactively about our finances, sacrificing a bit financially now, and doing some hard work on ourselves, we can position ourselves to move decisively toward our dreams when the time arrives. Even if we don't wind up making the specific change we envision, we still can leave ourselves better positioned to handle unforeseen circumstances that might arise, to indulge new desires that might materialize, or to enjoy more financial security.

Ultimately, planning for a Great Money Reset is about building more financial resilience and maximizing the opportunities open to us down the road. By taking responsibility now for our own future happiness, we can increase the odds that we'll feel empowered and in control of our destinies later on. Going long worked for my father. It works for many of my podcast listeners. It can work for *you*.

Which Are You, FIRE or FINE?

Callers to my podcast don't always speak of resilience, but they do often ask questions aimed at prepping themselves well in advance of a potential Great Money Reset. Take Mike from Michigan. When he called me in the late winter of 2021, he told me he envisioned wishing to step off the corporate treadmill in five or six years. Mike and his wife, Chantal, were both fifty-two years old, and they had two high-school-age kids. Chantal had recently bailed on her full-time job as a physician (yes, another case of pandemic-related burnout) and was working only one to two days a week on a contract basis, pulling in around $50,000 a year. Mike did well in his job, earning a salary of $250,000. He wanted to support Chantal's decision but worried that without her bigger paycheck he wouldn't be able to afford to make his own Great Money Reset when he wanted to. What could he do to prepare now so that he could switch up his life later?

Mike was actually in a pretty good situation. He and Chantal had socked away funds for their kids' college educations and had $2 million in retirement accounts as well as $300,000 in non-retirement savings. As I told Mike, his task over the next five years was to put away as much non-retirement savings as he could, preferably doubling that $300,000. Then, when those five years were up and Mike was ready to make his Great Money Reset, he and Chantal would have to commit to earning enough between them to cover their household bills. Assuming that they were spending $125,000 each year and Chantal was continuing to earn $50,000, Mike would have to find a new job that paid at least $75,000 and that also provided healthcare benefits.

It might have been nicer if Mike didn't have to work at all, but he had options. He could continue working in his present field but as a consultant; he could get a lower-stress and lower-paid job in his field; or he could take a lower-paid but more enjoyable job in a different field. Or perhaps Chantal would decide that she wanted to up the number of hours she was working or take on a second job. Whatever the case, if he and Chantal could cover their expenses and provide for healthcare, and if they had non-retirement assets to draw on in case they needed them, they would be in good shape. When they retired fully at, say, age sixty-seven, they would have a pile of retirement money as well as Social Security payments to draw on and would enjoy the kind of lifestyle to which they had become accustomed.

Since the pandemic, many people have become like Mike. Rather than just trudge along in the lives they have created for themselves, they want to be more deliberate, taking steps *now*—including those that require a bit of sacrifice—to ensure more opportunity later. One of my callers shared an acronym for this behavior: FINE, or Financial Independence, New Endeavor. It's a riff off of an existing movement called FIRE, or Financial Independence, Retire Early. In the aftermath of the Great Recession, a subculture arose among workers in their twenties and thirties around the notion that you didn't have to muddle through a traditional career for decades until you finally retired in your mid-sixties. Instead, by adopting a radical program of intense saving and monkish living, you could achieve financial independence and retire decades earlier—in your early fifties, forties, or even thirties.

Proponents of FIRE tended to break with the consumerism that has dominated American culture, prioritizing instead control over their time. If you could live without all the accoutrements of middle- and upper-class life—the expensive cars, the big house in the suburbs, the clothes, the shoes— you could gain something much more important: your freedom. Since the advent of the pandemic, this same impulse still seems to exist, but in a mutated form. Instead of seeking to make a clean break with the world of work, many people who call my show aim for something less extreme—a bit more control over their time and work conditions. Having questioned their old lives, they've concluded that they want to work less or differently, enjoy more flexibility in their jobs, work at a less stressful job, or shift to a new career. They don't necessarily wish to forgo the comforts of life, but they are willing to make at least some financial sacrifices in order to do it. They're thinking about their "next endeavor," and they want to achieve enough financial independence to make it great.

How can you become part of the FINE movement? As Mike's story suggests, it starts with a bit of basic financial planning five to ten years before your anticipated Great Money Reset. First, take a look at your spending and project forward. In your next endeavor, do you anticipate spending at the same rate or will you change your lifestyle? If you are willing, don't just say that—determine exactly which changes you anticipate making and how much you will save. Will you downsize your house? Will you forgo those fancy European trips each year? Will you pull your kids from private school? Will you make do with one car instead of two? How much of a difference will those shifts make to your monthly nut?

Next, look at your savings. How much money do you already have, and how much will you need down the road? If you're planning on making your Great Money Reset when you're in your late fifties, will you need to tap some of your savings to bridge the gap between then and when you would begin collecting Social Security or a pension? Will those savings suffice, or will you have to continue to generate some income? If you're in your forties and planning a next endeavor, will you still be able to contribute as much for retirement or your kids' college as you'll need? If you're in your thirties, will you have enough to help you buy your first house?

If you're in your twenties or thirties and thinking of quitting a job as part of a money reset, you'll want to consider how you'll replace any retirement benefits you might have been receiving. If your employer currently blesses you with an 8 percent match on your retirement contributions, can you save now to make up for missing that later? If you happen to work at a job that offers a pension, that might impact the timing of your Great Money Reset. If you were thinking of quitting your job in three years but you won't qualify for your pension for another five, or if you'll qualify for a larger pension in five, you'll want to suck it up if you can and wait it out.

Most people preparing for a next endeavor or major money reset will want to beef up their non-retirement accounts, even if it means contributing less to their retirement accounts. That might sound shocking, but as I've been saying all along, you need cash if you are going to make a big move. If you already have sufficient retirement funds saved up, start socking away more cash. Another common planning move is to pay off some of your future obligations now if you have the money. If you're in your early forties and have received a big bonus or other windfall and are planning a new endeavor, perhaps you'll want to front-load contributions to your children's 529 accounts. That way, you can take the need to save for college entirely off the table.

Ask yourself if there are any other potentially big financial obligations that you can imagine taking on in the future. Will your elderly parents or other relatives require any financial assistance from you? That might not be fun to think about, but it pays to be realistic. Sit down with your parents and learn about their financial situations. Think about any health issues they might have and whether they will be able to finance the care they'll need. If you have siblings, determine whether they plan to contribute or whether it will all be on you. Thinking about these issues now and planning for them will allow you to feel more confident when it comes time to undertake your next endeavor, and it will lower the odds of a nasty surprise.

Plan for the Worst-Case Scenarios

A friend of mine—I'll call him Steven—had a father who for years had owned and operated a marina in Rhode Island. It was a modest place, with aging equipment, a ragtag staff, and a small, run-down clubhouse that served crappy food and plenty of ice-cold beer on tap. In recent years, more affluent boaters had left for a more modern marina nearby that offered better amenities. Steven's sister Shelley helped their father with their clubhouse and other parts of the business, while Steven and another sister, Mindy, worked jobs of their own and were financially independent.

In 2020, Steven's father died suddenly of COVID. The tragedy set off a raging conflict in the family over what to do with the marina. The business itself wasn't worth much. Still, the real estate that it occupied was worth a considerable sum, about $1.5 million, with no mortgage. Shelley wanted their mother to keep the business so that she could continue to operate it. She felt that she deserved it, as she'd helped keep it running all of these years. Her plan was to pay her siblings their shares of the inheritance over time.

Mindy didn't like this idea. While Shelley had worked

in the marina over the years, Mindy didn't think her sister could run it without taking on a partner to manage the finances, and she doubted that taking on a partner was economically viable. Steven didn't like the idea, either, but for different reasons. Their mother was a seventy-three-year-old and in fairly good shape both physically and financially. After spending decades working as a teacher, she had a pension she could fall back on as well as Social Security. Those two checks just about covered her monthly needs. But as Steven argued, the family didn't know what life would hold in store for their mom. The kids had a responsibility to provide for her now, while they had the resources. The smartest choice would be to sell the marina and keep the proceeds for their mother to use as she aged if she needed them.

Since the children couldn't decide what to do, they let their mother have the final word. She was, in a word, gobsmacked. She didn't want to side with any of her children and risk alienating any of the others. For a while she struggled with the decision. Finally, she consulted her deceased husband's best friend, who told her that her husband would have wanted her to take care of herself. "For the first time in your life," he said, "you're going to have to behave a little selfishly and trust that your kids will be fine." That word, "selfish," rang in her ears—that was the last thing she wanted to be. In the end, though, she decided to sell the property, save a portion of the money for a rainy day, and hire someone to manage another chunk for the longer term. She reasoned that if she wound up not needing the money, it would ultimately pass to the kids. The decision did indeed alienate Shelley. To this day, she doesn't speak with her siblings.

I tell this story not to illuminate what to do when you leave behind a piece of real estate. Rather, I want to drill home a simple point: *You'd darn well better contemplate the end of your life and create an estate plan as part of your Great Money Reset.* My previous book discussed just how essential wills, powers of attorney, and healthcare proxies are, probably to the point of being annoying. But with all due humility, I was speaking the truth. Steven's parents had wills, but since they hadn't bothered to update them in thirty years and had never discussed them with anyone, no plan existed for how the kids would dispose of the marina and its real estate. A rift ensued that Steven's parents might have avoided.

If you're thinking about a big life change, consider the bad stuff that could happen and take simple steps to avoid it. I feel like a nagging aunt saying this to you, but so many people who otherwise are conscientious about planning for their next endeavor forget to think about the "What if I die?" question. They don't think about wills, and they don't think about getting the proper life insurance in place, either. You want to quit your $500,000 corporate law job to write poetry? Go for it. But in addition to making sure you've got the funds to pay your bills and save for your school-age kid's college education, make sure that you have insurance in place to secure your family's future. If your employer offers you a chance to buy life insurance at a reduced rate, you might want to apply for it before you undertake your next endeavor.

There's another question to ask and plan for: "What if I get sick?" You might come down with long COVID or some other dreaded disease, and what then? If you work for a large company, you might well have disability insurance to fall back on, but if you're planning to quit that corporate job and become a freelancer, you'll need to buy that insurance for yourself. Even more important, you'll need to ensure that you and your family have the proper health insurance in place. That means either deciding to work enough hours at a formal job to qualify for employer-subsidized insurance, or researching what it would cost to buy coverage and ensuring that you'll have enough saved up to cover the costs yourself.

Worst-case scenarios depress us, which is why so many of us don't like to think about them. But you don't want to wind up in a situation like Steven's family, do you? You don't want to get sick or have your spouse get sick a few years after your Great Money Reset and have inadequate health coverage. Bad stuff doesn't just happen to other people. Sometimes it happens to us. Take steps now in your planning, and you'll be prepared.

Why You Shouldn't Just Do It

Many people talk about Financial Independence, Retire Early, but they have trouble actually executing on it. Some struggle to maintain the Spartan lifestyle that FIRE generally requires. My caller John from Tennessee and his wife,

Maggie, had a different challenge. As John told me, he and Maggie spent years keeping their spending in check and "saving really hard," becoming accustomed to a simple, low-cost lifestyle. Now both of them were thirty-eight years old and near the end of their FIRE trajectory. They brought in a combined $185,000 each year and had no debt remaining except for $25,000 in student loans. Their $300,000 house was paid off. They had amassed $60,000 in their emergency fund, representing about a year's worth of expenses. They also had $380,000 in Roth IRAs, $820,000 in 401(k) accounts, and $600,000 in non-retirement savings.

In financial terms, John and Maggie had reached an amazing place—their dreams of early retirement were at hand. But they were in a different place emotionally, uncertain whether they should go through with their plans. John felt inclined to do so. He had spent fourteen years at his company and had become impatient with the politics inside his organization. He was ready for a change but still uncertain. Rather than retire outright, he thought maybe he would work a part-time, "fun" job to bring a little money in and obtain health insurance. Maggie was even more nervous about retiring. If John decided to leave his present job, she was thinking of continuing to work, bringing in her $65,000 salary. It was evidently too scary to think of making a clean break with the working world.

As John and Maggie's situation suggests, FIRE can sometimes burn too hot and fast for our own good, launching us into retirement before we feel ready. Indeed, something similar holds for any kind of major money reset—we might be able to figure out the dollars and cents part, but we forget about the emotional part, which can be just as important. A lack of funds can impede us from moving toward our dreams, but so can anxiety and a lack of confidence in our decision making.

Let's face it—personal change of any kind is *hard*, no matter how emotionally attuned we perceive ourselves to be. Dr. Sharon Melnick is a business psychologist, author, and executive coach who has worked with clients at many large companies. As she's found, people often make conscious decisions not to make a big change because the benefits of sticking with the status quo serve their long-term interests. Maybe they want to wait until their kids go off to school, or they don't want to disrupt their partner's lucrative and satisfying career, or they like their current level of life balance, or they're eligible for some financial reward—a big bonus or stock award—and want to wait for that.[1]

Many other times, though, people avoid change without even realizing it simply because they're scared of losing financial security, their relationships, even their sense of identity. As we've seen, pursuing change can entail risking a level of prosperity and stability we've already achieved. It can test important relationships in our lives or cause them to evolve in unpredictable ways. We might also see our job or some other aspect of our present situation as part of ourselves,

---

1 Dr. Sharon Melnick, interview with the author, January 13, 2022.

perceiving any change as disorienting and a potential aban-
donment of selfhood. The potential for loss in these areas is
just as real as the potential for positive growth—and quite
scary. For some of us, our fear of loss grows so large as to be
downright paralyzing. We might also harbor a generalized
fear of the unknown, feeling reluctant to venture beyond a
current reality that feels comfortable and familiar.

Mindset also can come into play. People might have a scar-
city mindset that prevents them from changing their current
circumstances. They might presume that money or opportunities are in short supply, making it seem unwise to risk what
they already have. Referencing the work of the influential psychologist Carol Dweck, Melnick notes that many people are
hobbled by a "fixed" mindset, believing that they're stuck
with the skills or abilities that they have innately. They don't
orient themselves toward experimenting or envisioning new
opportunities, and they resist when others impose change on
them. They might avoid thinking about change, claiming that
they're "too busy" to spend time considering what retirement
or some other future stage holds for them.

People who succeed in making big, weighty changes in
their lives manage to think their way past such sources of re-
sistance. They bring change out from *within*, often thanks to
conscious effort on their part. Well before they actually quit
their jobs, move clear across the country, or become engaged
to get married, they spend months or years envisioning it,
thinking it through, coming to terms with any sacrifices or

losses involved, and evolving as people in ways that support the change. They ask and answer tough questions about their life goals and arrive at a place of clarity. Conversely, when we don't allow enough time for a process of introspection to occur, often we either don't manage to go through with big changes, or we make changes that lead us in the wrong direction and fail to make us any happier. We remain where we don't want to be—stuck.

Take Beth, a corporate executive making about a half million dollars a year. She was deeply unhappy in her job and eager to make a change. Her friends worried that she was drinking more than she had in the past, possibly on account of a nasty divorce she'd been through. One day, a headhunter called and offered her a plum job at a European company that would triple her salary. Beth had felt underpaid given her talents and experience, so she was tempted to take the job. Her friends weren't so sure. The company was in turmoil, and the headquarters was known to be a chaotic place. She'd have to move to Belgium, where she lacked a strong social network. Although the bump in pay would be a nice ego boost, Beth might struggle without her friends nearby. Single with no kids, she already had more than enough money to fund her lifestyle.

Beth took the job and, sad to say, it didn't end well. Within ten months, she had three different bosses. The third boss fired her, not because Beth had underperformed but simply because he wanted to clean house. Beth moved back home and was able to find a new job at a company in a different industry. Her unhappiness grew, however, as did her drinking, to the point where she had to take a leave of absence. She got treatment for her addiction and continued to recover at home. While she now is sober, those dark years haunt her.

Let Beth's example be a lesson to us. We can quit our jobs in a quest for happiness. We can move halfway around the world. We can get divorced. We can start new relationships. We can go back to school. But unless we've done the challenging emotional work required to grow as people, all of that change remains superficial. We're merely transporting our old problems to new places.

Beth yearned for a change, but she didn't take the time to define her dreams by considering what she really wanted and needed to be happy. In her case, doing so might have been too painful, forcing her to dredge up and process painful demons from her youth. But if she had managed to look inward, she might have concluded that taking the new job was precisely the wrong move. Maybe she could have found a way to improve her current job—for instance, by approaching her current boss and asking for a pay boost.

Maybe she would have decided to take a period of time away from work to learn more about herself and develop hobbies and interests that she had neglected. Maybe she could have found an entirely different career path on which to embark (interestingly enough, she had taught a college course once as an adjunct professor and loved it, but hadn't pursued it further). Or maybe she would have prompted herself to get treatment months or years earlier for her alcoholism, which in turn might have addressed her problems earlier and saved her from excess suffering.

Go Build a Wall

How can we emotionally prepare for a Great Money Reset so we don't do what Beth did—take a blind and perhaps misguided leap at the first seemingly attractive opportunity? Many of us could no doubt stand to work with a therapist and go deep into our feelings, unraveling the issues that might have kept us stuck in the past and that might still do so in the present. Coaching can help—Melnick, for instance, routinely works with corporate leaders to help them get unstuck and move more decisively toward their dreams.

We can also take steps on our own. Larry Shushansky, a Rhode Island–based therapist in private practice who often works with people who are stuck, emphasizes the importance of changing our habits little by little as a prelude to making big, fundamental changes. The first step, he counsels, is to adopt a goal for ourselves and truly commit to it. The nature and extent of this commitment is key: We must develop a deep-seated belief that if we achieve this particular goal, our life will be better for it, despite the potential adversity we may experience.

With a firm commitment in place, we must try moving incrementally toward our goal, taking small steps at first. We should keep working at our goal day after day, week after week, sticking with this process of change as long as it takes. Referencing the concept of neuroplasticity, Shushansky holds that a gradualist approach doesn't simply habituate us to change. Over time, it actually creates new pathways in our brains, locking in new, more desirable patterns of thought that set us up for the bigger changes we seek.[2]

As an example of how this works, Shushansky tells the story of a client of his, a senior executive at a large firm, who was immensely successful but also miserable in his job. This executive—Kurt—was tempted to quit his job straight away and retire, but his boss told him to take some time off to figure out his next move. Kurt agreed.

What he did next might seem odd at first glance. Kurt arranged for a company to deliver truckloads of stone to his backyard. Kurt liked working with his hands, and he had always dreamed of building a stone wall. Now, finally, he was going to do it. Kurt's friends and family thought he was nuts. This wall would be an eyesore, messing up a beautiful backyard on which Kurt had already spent a small fortune. Kurt also had no idea how to build a wall. But after talking through these and other obstacles with his therapist, Kurt resolved to move ahead. For him, building the wall served as an exercise in doing exactly what he wanted to do, instead of what he or others thought he *should* do.

---

2 Larry Shushansky, interview with the author, January 24, 2022.

Kurt researched construction techniques, planned out the wall, and set about building it on his property. Day after day, he put in eight hours of backbreaking work. Some days, he would look at a section of wall he'd been working on, feel dissatisfied with it, take that section down, and redo it. Other days, he felt proud of what he'd accomplished. The daily work took a toll on his body—he had never done such intense manual labor before. But as the weeks passed, Kurt learned how to stretch his muscles and pick up heavy stone in ways that allowed him to avoid injury. He also learned how to listen to his body and take breaks when he needed them.

After about three months, Kurt finished his wall. He also knew exactly what he wanted his next move to be. Big surprise: It wasn't retirement. Rather, he decided that he would leave his leadership role at the company and go back to working in a lower-level sales job. He had worked for years in sales, and he'd loved it. Now he would have a chance to recoup all that he had missed in recent years: the chance to build relationships, to help customers address their problems, to immerse himself in the technical aspect of the company's products. Would he have to take a pay cut? Would he lose stature in the company? Absolutely. But because he had taken the time to process these losses and to learn to think about himself in a different way, the shift didn't seem so scary. It just seemed right.

Kurt nearly made the same mistake Beth did—rushing headlong into a big change before he was emotionally prepared. Instead, he took his time. Working on the wall gave Kurt the solitude he needed as well as an initial sense of what it might feel like to live more authentically, on *his* terms. During his time off, he continued to explore his situation with Shushansky in therapy, working to define what he wanted out of life, to identify the obstacles that were impeding his happiness, and to come up with solutions that would increase his happiness without damaging his personal relationships. As a result of these combined efforts, Kurt didn't simply change his circumstances, he changed himself.

As Shushansky observes, real, deep change isn't a singular event. It's a process, a series of actions that we take in the world that also translate into an evolution in our thinking and self-perception. This process doesn't end, by the way, once we gain newfound clarity. It keeps going. In Kurt's case, the growth process continued as he went about bringing his new plan to fruition. He had conversations with his wife and kids, getting them on board with his decision and the financial sacrifices that it would entail. He had multiple conversations with his boss, the company's CEO, to convince him to let him make this move. Each concrete step built upon and solidified the clarity he had come to while building his wall.

Just as we should perform financial planning for a big move months or years in advance, so we should set out on this process of emotional change. We don't know where it might lead us. Maybe we'll wind up making the Great Money Reset we envisioned at the outset. Maybe we'll go in a different direction. Maybe we'll find an entirely new way to experience and appreciate our present circumstances. Whatever the case, when we reach that future point, we'll have positioned ourselves both financially and emotionally to embark on the next phase of our lives.

This book has focused on the financial side of making a Great Money Reset. We've covered all the basics—running through the dollars and cents, rethinking your spending, bullying your boss, making the right investment moves, working the tax laws to your advantage, taking stock of real estate, considering your educational options and whether you should start or sell a business, and mobilizing family support. In this last chapter, we've examined the virtues of laying the financial groundwork for future Great Money Resets. All along, I've tried to help empower those who might feel fearful or reluctant to undergo a big change by helping them to think through how to make it more financially practicable.

And yet, as I hope you can see, a Great Money Reset isn't fundamentally about money. It's about rethinking our *lives*. Money is just the vehicle. Like Kurt's stone wall, money gives us a tangible means of approaching and apprehending our intangible feelings. Any fears or resistances we harbor toward changing our lives likely run deep—much deeper than anxiety about a diminished retirement or lower standard of living. If you're already in tune with your feelings, thinking about money can help you affirm, refine, and solidify what you already know about yourself. If your emotions are still somewhat murky, contemplating the dollars and cents can prompt you in turn to ask tough questions of yourself. Either way, you'll be more empowered to overcome any fears you might have and take a risk.

I do hope you're more excited about a Great Money Reset than you were when first opening this book. After all, life is so short, and few regrets loom so large as the opportunities you *didn't* take, the boldness you *didn't* show. If you have aspirations or ambitions you've long subdued, I urge you to take them seriously. Don't chain yourself to what is comfortable and familiar. Don't satisfy yourself with the usual distractions. Take a chance. Strike out in a new direction. Do it intelligently, thoughtfully, deliberately, and incrementally. You *can* turn upheaval into opportunity. And you owe it to yourself and those around you to try.

I, for one, can't wait to see what you achieve.

Rock the Reset

- Start planning five to ten years before a potential life or career change, looking at spending, savings, your financial goals, and financial obligations you might have. Be sure to plan for worst-case scenarios.

- Prepare emotionally for big shifts. Real change can only truly take root if it starts from within.

- A Great Money Reset isn't fundamentally about money. It's about rethinking our *lives*. Money is just the vehicle.

Acknowledgments

After finishing my first book, I told anyone who would listen, "One and done. I will never write another book." So much for that. The band is back, starting with Seth Schulman, who can focus my attention and hone my words like nobody else. Working with Seth is like dancing with an old partner who knows where I will be going before I do.

My agent, Brian DeFiore, never believed me when I said I couldn't write a second book. As always, his clear thinking, sound judgment, and high tolerance for my histrionics helped this project take its form.

George Witte, editor in chief of St. Martin's Publishing Group, was an early fan of the Great Money Reset concept and trusted me to use my voice, while organizing and prioritizing the information and advice. George asks all the right questions, and usually already has the answers. I am grateful as well to his colleagues Laura Clark, Sara Beth Haring, Tracey Guest, and Brigitte Dale for helping me to craft the book's message in smart, thought-provoking ways.

Michael Goodman, CPA/PFS, CFP®, read early drafts

of this book and helped to keep me on my technical toes. Sherry King took long walks with me and my dogs in Riverside Park, listening as I recounted stories that would make it into the book. She was also kind enough to read and edit the manuscript. Michael Stein took time out from his life as a doctor and author to ensure that what I had written sounded like "the real Jill."

My inner-circle pal Maureen was integral in my own Great Money Reset almost fifteen years ago. Her wife, Andrea, continues to wow me with her adaptability and positive attitude, both of which helped to spark early ideas for the book. I also owe a debt of gratitude to Dr. Sharon Melnick, whom I met on the soccer field four decades ago, before she became a superstar academic, author, and executive coach. A big thank-you goes out to three others who participated in the project— Larry Shushansky, Cheri Ruane, Robbie Abed—as well as to the many faux and real nieces and nephews who told me at length about what it was like to reset their lives.

I'd like to send a special shout-out to Spencer Brown, who helped launch the *Jill on Money* podcast and has been a voice of reason over the decades since I was in his wedding party. I also want to extend my gratitude to the callers and viewers who speak to me every day and allow me to participate in their own Great Money Resets.

Professionally, I would never be where I am today without the early coaching and encouragement of Betty-Jo Cugini and Bill Hess, the first two people who thought that I could make the leap into journalism from financial planning and money management. Harvey Nagler and Constance Lloyd at CBS helped me to create the *Jill on Money* radio show, and their successor, Craig Swagler, continues to provide advice, guidance, and friendship.

The love of my parents, sister, and brother-in-law have always anchored me, giving me the strength and confidence to reset my own life. They were paragons of support as my life took twists and turns that I never could have imagined.

And of course, Jackie, my partner and muse, has always been a beacon of rational thought and provider of unconditional love. I promised her that I would try not to swear in this book, which I mostly accomplished!

Index